W9-CAR-377

Better Homes and Gardens®
STEP-BY-STEP
Basic Carpentry

Better Homes and Gardens® Books
Des Moines, Iowa

Series: Better Homes and Gardens
Carpentry.
Building.

Better Homes and Gardens® Books
An imprint of Meredith® Books

Step-by-Step Basic Carpentry
Editor: Benjamin W. Allen
Associate Art Director: Tom Wegner
Copy Chief: Angela K. Renkoski
Copy Editor: James Sanders
Electronic Production Coordinator: Paula Forest
Editorial Assistants: Susan McBroom, Karen Schirm, Barbara Suk
Design Assistant: Jennifer Norris
Production Director: Douglas M. Johnston
Production Manager: Pam Kvitne
Prepress Coordinator: Marjorie J. Schenkelberg

Meredith® Books
Editor in Chief: James D. Blume
Design Director: Matt Strelecki
Managing Editor: Gregory H. Kayko
Executive Shelter Editor: Denise L. Caringer
Vice President, General Manager: Jamie L. Martin

Better Homes and Gardens® **Magazine**
Editor in Chief: Jean LemMon
Executive Building Editor: Joan McCloskey

Meredith Publishing Group
President, Publishing Group: Christopher M. Little
Vice President and Publishing Director: John P. Loughlin

Meredith Corporation
Chairman of the Board: Jack D. Rehm
President and Chief Executive Officer: William T. Kerr
Chairman of the Executive Committee: E. T. Meredith III

Produced by Greenleaf Publishing, Inc.
Publishing Director: Dave Toht
Associate Editor: Steve Cory
Assistant Editor: Rebecca JonMichaels
Design: Melanie Lawson Design
Illustrations: Brian Gilmer, Art Factory
Technical Consultant: Ches Olson

Cover photograph: Tony Kubat Photography

All of us at Better Homes and Gardens® Books are dedicated to providing you with information and
ideas you need to enhance your home. We welcome your comments and suggestions about this
book on carpentry. Write to us at: Better Homes and Gardens® Books, Do-It-Yourself Editorial
Department, RW–206, 1716 Locust St., Des Moines, IA 50309–3023.

Note to the Reader: Due to differing conditions, tools, and individual skills, Meredith Corporation
assumes no responsibility for any damages, injuries suffered, or losses incurred as a result of
following the information published in this book. Before beginning any project, review the
instructions carefully, and if any doubts or questions remain, consult local experts or authorities.
Because local codes and regulations vary greatly, you always should check with local authorities to
ensure that your project complies with all applicable local codes and regulations. Always read and
observe all of the safety precautions provided by any tool or equipment manufacturer, and follow all
accepted safety procedures.

TABLE OF CONTENTS

INTRODUCTION

Many people think that carpentry projects can be handled only by professionals with years of experience. As a result, they pay hundreds and even thousands of dollars to contractors, not knowing if they are getting a fair price or quality workmanship. Other people believe carpentry projects can be tackled by anyone. They plunge into projects they are not prepared to handle. The results often are disastrous. A person with little or no experience will not be able to cut a straight line, much less construct a wall or build a cabinet. Basic carpentry skills are within reach of any homeowner, but they require instruction and practice. If you take the time to learn the basics well, you will be able to succeed at a variety of carpentry jobs.

Step-by-Step Carpentry explains how wood structures are put together and what it takes to tackle most repairs and improvements. This book will show you, one step at a time, how to fix minor and major problems and how to build new walls, ceilings, and floors. Many other projects also are included. Once you have learned basic carpentry techniques, you can save money by doing projects yourself—and you'll experience the satisfaction of completing well-built structures with your own hands. Even when you choose to pay someone to do work you feel is beyond your skill level, you'll be able to make sure that the job has been done right and at a fair price.

Working to Code

Although you may be an amateur working on your own house, you have the same responsibilities to building authorities as a licensed carpenter. Any structure you build must be solid and long-lasting, plumb and square, and must be constructed of materials appropriate for the job. That means using only those techniques and materials that meet your local building codes.

The procedures in this book will satisfy most local codes, but be aware that codes can vary widely. Always check with your city or county building department if you are considering adding to or changing the structure of your house in any substantial way or if you believe your existing structures might be substandard.

Building codes may seem bothersome, but they are designed to make your home safe and worry-free. Ignoring codes can lead to costly mistakes, health hazards, and even difficulties in someday selling your house. Minor repairs do not require permits. However, changes involving framing; major projects, such as kitchen or bath remodelings or adding a new room; or any job affecting plumbing and electrical systems typically require permits. If you are in any doubt, check with your building department before proceeding. Neglecting to do so could cause you the expense and trouble of tearing out and redoing work. (In the course of completing carpentry work, you will expose wiring and pipes. Take a little time to make sure these systems are safe and up to code before you cover them up again.)

There's no telling what kind of building inspector you will encounter when you apply for your permit or when they inspect your site: Some can be helpful, friendly, and flexible; others are real nitpickers. No matter who you deal with, your work will go better if you follow these guidelines:

■ To avoid unnecessary questions about your plans, seek out as much information as possible and incorporate that information into your plan before you take it in for approval. Your building department may have literature explaining requirements for the type of project you have planned.

■ Go to your building department with a plan to be approved or amended; don't expect its inspectors to plan the job for you. Present your plan with neatly drawn diagrams and a complete list of the materials you will be using.

■ Be sure you understand clearly at what stages of your project you need to have inspections. Do not cover up any work that needs to be inspected.

■ Be as courteous as possible. Inspectors often are wary of homeowners because so many do shoddy work. Show the inspector you are serious about doing things the correct way.

How to Use This Book

Begin by reading "Getting to Know Your Home" on pages 6–7. This provides general knowledge to help you understand specific parts of your home's structure. Then, read the next section, "Tools and Materials," to choose the tools you need or want and to get acquainted with the lumber and hardware that is available to you.

Look through the section on "Carpentry Techniques" to get an idea of the basic procedures involved in most carpentry projects. When the need arises, you can refer back to these pages. The final section, "Carpentry Projects," discusses specific projects; there is no need to read about these until you plan to undertake one of those projects.

Feature Boxes

In addition to basic instructions, you'll find plenty of tips throughout the book. For every project, a "You'll Need" box tells you how long the project will take, what skills are necessary, and what tools you must have. The other tip boxes shown on this page provide practical help to ensure that the carpentry work you do will be as pleasurable as possible, and that it will result in safe, long-lasting improvements to your home.

MEASUREMENTS

Keep an eye out for this box when standard measurements, critical tolerances, or special measuring techniques are called for.

Money $ Saver

Throwing money at a job does not necessarily make it a better one. Money Saver helps cut your costs with tips on how to accurately estimate your material needs, make wise tool purchases, and organize the job to minimize wasted labor.

EXPERTS' INSIGHT

Tricks of the trade can make all the difference in helping you do a job quickly and well. Experts' Insight gives insiders' tips on methods and materials that make the job easier.

CAUTION!

When a how-to step requires special care, Caution! warns you what to watch out for. It will help keep you from doing damage to yourself or the job at hand.

TOOLS TO USE

If you'll need special tools not commonly found in a homeowner's toolbox, we'll tell you about them in Tools to Use.

GETTING TO KNOW YOUR HOME

When you plan a carpentry project or go to a building supply center for materials, it helps to know the common terms describing the parts of your house. Some of these terms vary from region to region, but most are understood throughout the country. Although this book deals primarily with interior carpentry projects, you need to be able to visualize how your house is put together. Even a task as simple as attaching a wall shelf or installing baseboard molding requires some knowledge of framing.

The house shown at *right* combines the elements of old and new construction—a situation you may find in your own home. The two-story section of the house shows construction methods and materials common between 1910 and 1960. The one-story addition shows materials and techniques in common use by contractors today.

Framing is the skeleton of your house, the basic structure holding it together. Vertical **wall studs** run from floor to ceiling. They're usually made of 2×4s, but often 2×6s or 2×8s are used to allow for more insulation. The horizontal pieces at the top and bottom of the walls are called **plates**. The bottom plate rests on a **concrete block** or **formed concrete** foundation. Walls may have **fire blocking** running horizontally about halfway up the wall.

Wherever there is an opening for a door or a window, a correctly sized **header**, made of a massive piece of lumber or two pieces of 2× lumber, must span the gap in the framing. For more details about framing, see pages 96–97.

Roofs are supported by either **rafters** or **trusses**, which use small-dimensioned lumber joined in such a way as to give them strength. **Collar ties** brace the rafters. The roof typically is made of plywood or shiplap covered with **roofing felt** and **shingles**. **Eaves** are trimmed with **fascia**. **Vents** draw hot air from the attic.

Joists made of 2×10s support **subfloors** and **flooring** and other interior load-bearing walls. The undersides of joists provide nailing surfaces for ceilings.

On the exterior walls, the framing is covered with at least three layers of material. First comes **sheathing**, which in older homes is made of 1× lumber run horizontally. When it's milled with an overlapping joint, it is called **shiplap**. Plywood, fiberboard, or foamboard is used in newer homes. Next comes a paperlike layer to improve insulation and reduce the effects of condensation. Older homes use **roofing felt** (also called tar paper) or a reddish-colored building paper; newer homes have **house wrap**, often made of polyethylene. Finally, the house is clad in siding. This house has horizontal **beveled siding**, but vertical siding and sheet siding are also common. Inside the walls, older homes often have gray-colored **rock wool insulation**; **fiberglass batts** are used now.

Interior wall surfaces of older homes usually are covered with **lath**, thin pieces of rough, ⅜-inch thick wood, run horizontally. The lath is covered with two or three layers of **plaster**. Today **drywall** is nailed or screwed to the framing and the joints and nail holes are covered with joint compound. Plastering is a specialized skill that takes years to learn, but a homeowner can apply and finish drywall (see pages 100–105).

Gaps around windows (**double-hung sash**, **casement**, **fixed-pane**, or **full-round**), doors, and along walls are covered with molding. See pages 38 and 72–75 for how to apply molding.

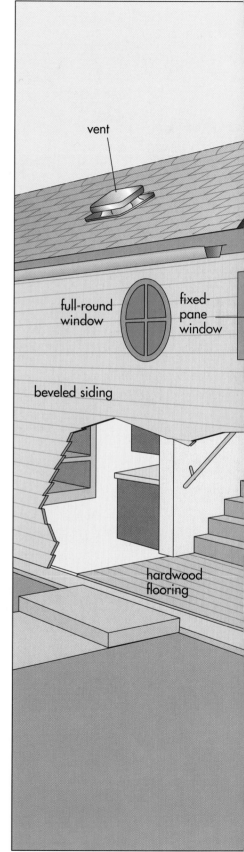

vent

full-round window

fixed-pane window

beveled siding

hardwood flooring

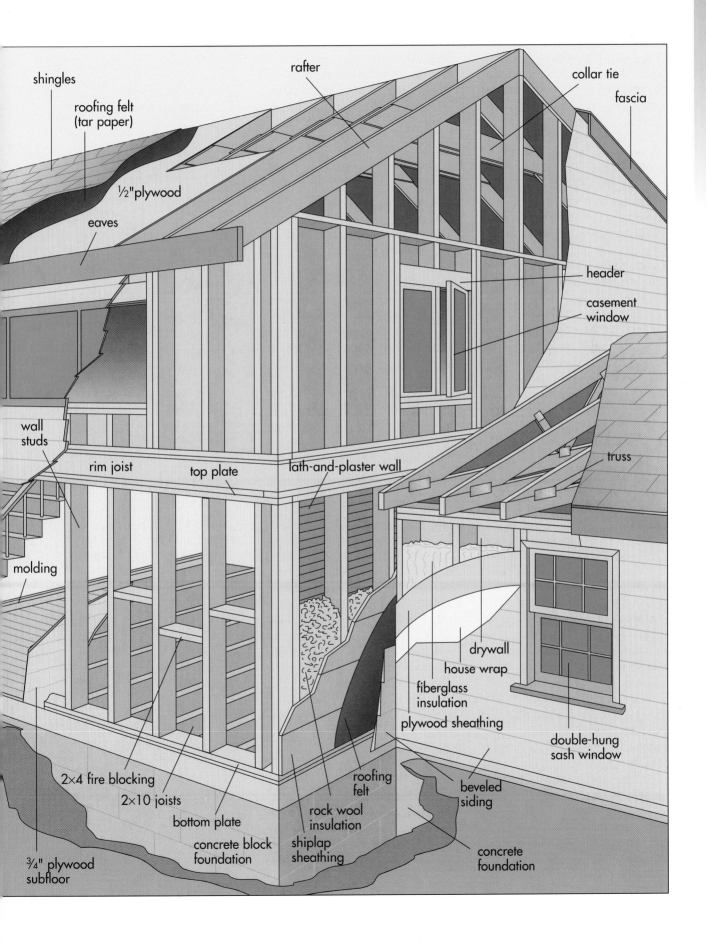

shingles

roofing felt
(tar paper)

rafter

collar tie

fascia

½"plywood

eaves

header

casement
window

wall
studs

rim joist

top plate

lath-and-plaster wall

truss

molding

drywall

house wrap

fiberglass
insulation

plywood sheathing

double-hung
sash window

2×4 fire blocking

2×10 joists

bottom plate

concrete block
foundation

roofing
felt

beveled
siding

¾" plywood
subfloor

rock wool
insulation

shiplap
sheathing

concrete
foundation

SELECTING HAND TOOLS

Often, the right hand tool makes your job easier and yields better results. Hand tools are relatively inexpensive so it's easy to gather quite a collection. To avoid becoming a tool junkie who fills the basement with tools that will never be used, assemble a basic tool kit and add to your collection only when the job at hand requires a new tool.

Typically, the top-of-the-line contractor-type tool model will be of higher quality than an average homeowner needs, but inexpensive tools will not perform well. Your best choice is a mid-priced model. If you need a tool to complete an unusual task and probably won't need it very often, go with the cheaper version.

Few tools see more action than the flexible **tape measure.** Buy a 25-foot one with a 1-inch-wide blade; this will extend farther and last longer than a ¾-inch one. Some carpenters prefer a folding ruler for smaller jobs. Purchase one with a metal pull-out extension for making precise inside-to-inside measurements (see page 28).

A **framing square** (also called a carpenter's square) is used to check corners for square and to mark for rafters and stringers. More often, you'll need a smaller square. A triangular **speed square** is easy to use, allows you to quickly figure 45-degree-angle cuts, and holds its shape after getting banged around. It slips into your back pocket and is handy for quickly marking cut lines on planks and framing material. A **combination square** is helpful for scribing lines (see page 29). A **T-bevel** can be set to duplicate an angle.

Plumb and level large and small projects with a **carpenter's level.** A 2- or 4-foot model works well for most projects. A **plumb bob**

establishes true vertical lines. Snap long, straight lines with a **chalk line.** A chalk line also can double as a plumb bob.

Although you will do most of your cutting with power tools, a **handsaw** still comes in handy. You may want to choose a smaller saw that fits into a tool box. For accurate miter cuts, use a **backsaw** and **miter box.** Use a **drywall saw** to cut curves in drywall. To make rough curved cuts in wood, choose a **keyhole saw.** Cut intricate and precise curves in thin materials with a **coping saw.**

Wood chisels enable you to shape mortises and make rough notches in places where a saw will not reach. Choose chisels with metal-capped handles. Have a **utility knife** close at hand for razor-sharp cuts. Most people prefer one with a retractable blade. To shave wood along the length of a board, use a **plane** for the smoothest cut. For final shaping, use a **rasp** or a **wood file.**

Buy a **hammer** that is comfortable and solidly built. The most popular model weighs 16 ounces and has curved claws. You'll find a baffling array of specialty hammers, including framing and wallboard hammers. Stick to the basic curved-claw hammer. To sink the heads of finishing nails below the surface of the work, use a **nail set.**

Have plenty of **screwdrivers** on hand; get various sizes of both Phillips-tipped and slot-tipped types, or buy a combination screwdriver that has four tips in one tool. Make pilot holes for small screws with an **awl.**

To fasten nuts, bolts, and lag screws, use an **adjustable wrench.** For holding pieces of wood firmly, have **C-clamps** of various sizes handy. A pair of **locking pliers** helps to hold fasteners or pieces of wood tight while you work.

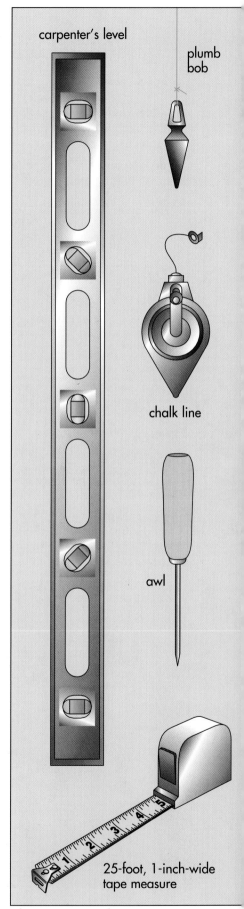

carpenter's level

plumb bob

chalk line

awl

25-foot, 1-inch-wide tape measure

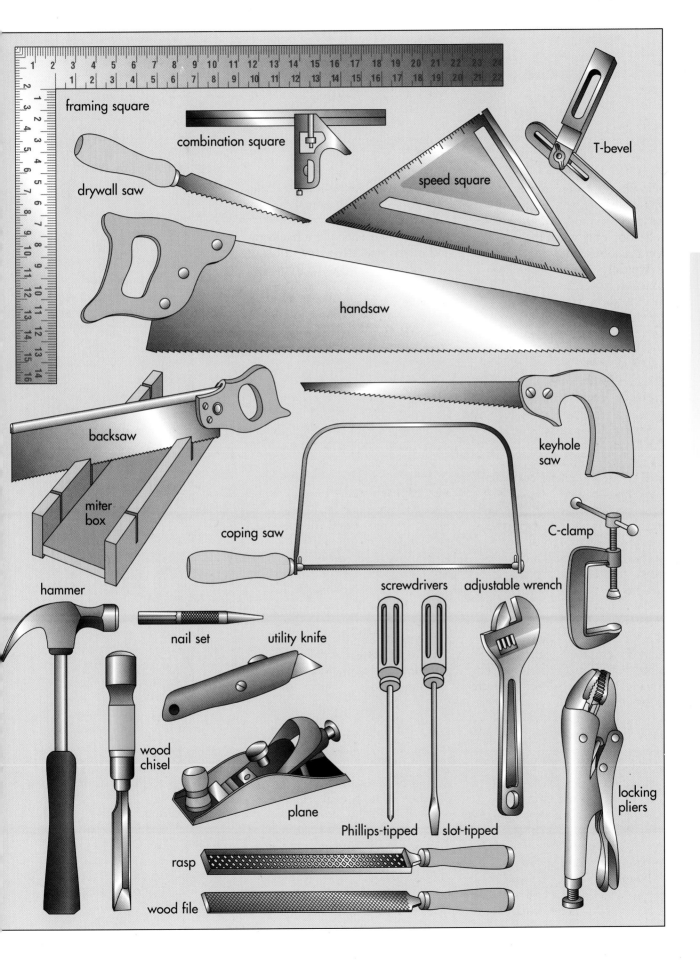

framing square

combination square

drywall saw

speed square

T-bevel

handsaw

backsaw

miter box

coping saw

keyhole saw

C-clamp

hammer

nail set

utility knife

screwdrivers

adjustable wrench

wood chisel

plane

Phillips-tipped

slot-tipped

locking pliers

rasp

wood file

Tongue-and-groove pliers are one of the most useful tools you can buy so it makes sense to pay extra for a high-quality pair. They grab most anything firmly and work well for pulling nails. **Lineman's pliers** enable you to grab things tightly from the front rather than the side of the tool and also will cut nails or screws. **Side-cutting pliers** enable you to cut nails nearly flush to the surface. They also are useful for grabbing the pointed ends of finish nails to pull them out of the back of molding without marring the face.

A **flat pry bar** is indispensable. With it, you can pry apart fastened lumber pieces with minimal damage to the wood. It also is handy for levering heavy objects into place; for example, reattaching a door on its hinges.

A **cat's paw** (also called a nail puller) makes it easy to pull nails, although it will damage the wood (see page 57). It's indispensable if you are planning any demolition.

For patching damaged walls and for taping drywall, have a variety of sizes of **taping knives** to apply wallboard compound (see pages 104–105). If you have 6-, 8-, and 12-inch blades you will be prepared to tape or patch most any surface. If you have a lot of drywall to cut, you'll thank yourself for buying a **drywall square.** You'll find it is also very useful for marking cut lines on pieces of plywood.

Sanding large wall and ceiling areas is much easier if you have a **pole sander.** Buy a smaller sanding block for detail work (see page 68).

Use a **caulking gun** to fill cracks with caulk or to apply construction adhesive. Purchase a **staple gun** to attach sheets of plastic or felt or to install fiberglass insulation batts.

A **forming tool** is easier to use than a plane for working wood, but it will not cut as straight or as smooth. It is more versatile, however, and comes in handy for fine-tuning anything from foam board to wallboard.

When you need to stabilize something that is too thick to handle with a C-clamp, use a quick-fitting **adjustable clamp.** To clamp a straightedge in place or hold thin materials that might be marred by a C-clamp (see pages 8–9) or adjustable clamp, use a **squeeze clamp** (see page 59 for other specialized clamps).

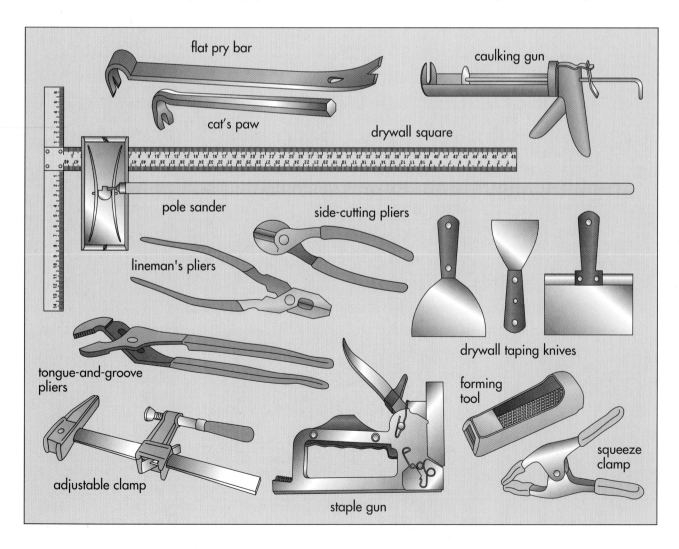

flat pry bar

caulking gun

cat's paw

drywall square

pole sander

side-cutting pliers

lineman's pliers

drywall taping knives

tongue-and-groove pliers

forming tool

adjustable clamp

squeeze clamp

staple gun

SELECTING BASIC POWER TOOLS

A circular saw, a power drill, and a sabersaw are musts for your basic tool kit. With the two saws you can make straight and curved cuts quickly in almost any material. The drill lets you make holes of almost any size and drive screws quickly and easily. With these three tools, you can handle most any household carpentry job.

A **circular saw** crosscuts, angle-cuts, rips (cuts lengthwise), and even bevels lumber easily and cleanly. Don't worry if the saw has a plastic housing; many plastics are very strong. Do take a look at the metal baseplate. A baseplate made of thin, stamped metal can warp; look for a thicker base made of extruded or cast metal. A saw that takes 7¼-inch blades is the usual choice. It lets you cut to a depth of about 2½ inches at 90 degrees and to cut through a piece of 2× lumber even when the blade is set at 45 degrees.

Horsepower is not important when choosing a circular saw. Instead, look at the amperage and the type of bearings. A low-cost saw pulls only 9 or 10 amps and runs on rollers or sleeve bearings. This means less power, a shorter life because it heats up easily, and less precise cuts because the blade wobbles somewhat. Better saws are rated at 12 or 13 amps and run on ball bearings. This combination of extra power and smoother operation makes for long life and more precise cutting. Worm-drive saws, which are the most powerful saws and have the longest-lasting bearings, are heavy and hard to use. As is often the case, a mid-priced saw is your best choice.

Be sure to get a variable-speed, reversible **power drill.** Unless you will be doing heavy-duty work, you don't need one with a ½-inch chuck; a ⅜-inch one is fine. Buy a drill that pulls at least 3.5 amps. A keyless chuck makes changing bits quick and easy, but some people prefer a keyed chuck for a tighter grip on the bit.

A **cordless drill** frees you to work without the mess of electrical cords. Buy one that uses at least 9.6 volts, preferably more. If possible, get an extra battery pack so you won't have to wait for a battery to charge.

When buying a **sabersaw,** examine the baseplate and the mechanism for adjusting it. On cheaper saws, these are flimsy and eventually wobble, making it difficult to keep the blade aligned vertically. Variable speed is a useful option. A saw pulling 3 amps or more handles most difficult jobs.

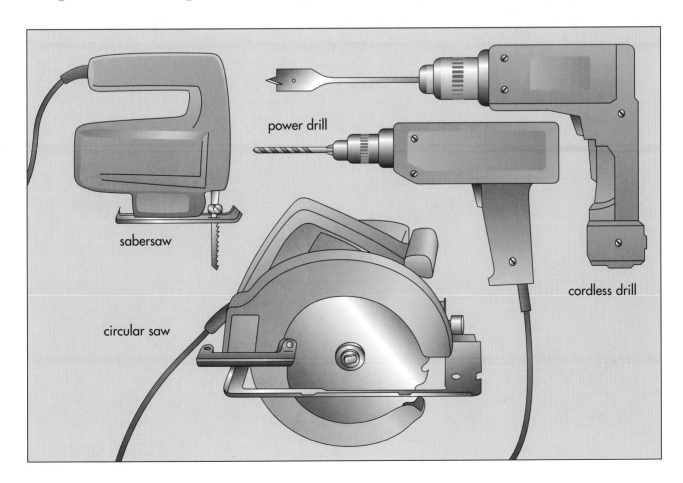

power drill

sabersaw

cordless drill

circular saw

SELECTING SPECIALIZED POWER TOOLS

The more carpentry jobs you take on, the more power tools you will need or want to own. Many of these are high-priced items, so do some careful research before making a purchase. If the tool is one you will turn to often, pay extra money to get a good-quality one that will last. If you will use it only rarely, settle for a lesser-quality tool.

To determine the quality of a tool, check the amperage rather than the horsepower. Compare models and avoid buying the one with the lowest amperage rating. A plastic housing is not necessarily a sign of poor quality. But do check any mechanisms and metal attachments to see if they're solid. A tool with ball bearings runs smoother and lasts longer than one with other types of bearings.

For quick sanding of large areas, nothing beats a **belt sander.** Make sure it uses belts that are easily available—3×24 inches is the most common size. A good belt sander is fairly heavy and has a large dust collector. You can switch from rough to fine sanding belts; however, because a belt sander is difficult to handle for fine work, you probably will want to use another method for the final sanding—either a hand-sanding block or a smaller mechanized sander, such as a **random-orbit** sander. It works by moving rapidly in small circles. Some people prefer the finish of an older-style vibrating sander, which simply moves back and forth. Some units switch from random-orbit to vibrating action.

With a **router,** you can mill lumber to a wide variety of shapes (see page 51). If you choose a solid model with plenty of power and a base that won't warp with age, you can produce pieces that are just as straight and smooth as millwork from a factory.

If you plan a project that calls for joining two pieces of lumber side by side, a **biscuit joiner** produces professional-looking

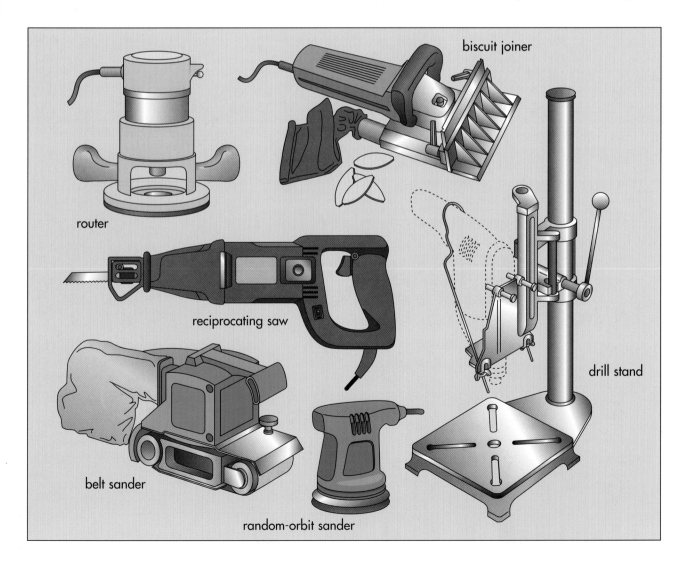

biscuit joiner

router

reciprocating saw

drill stand

belt sander

random-orbit sander

results with ease (see page 65).

Need to drill holes that are precisely vertical? You can purchase a drill press or a **drill stand** that uses a regular power drill. A stand is less expensive than a drill press, but does take more time to set up and use.

For demolition work, nothing beats a **reciprocating saw.** It can make cuts in places where no other saw will reach. If you need to remove portions of walls or floors, this tool can save you a lot of time and frustration.

If you have to cut a lot of molding or exterior siding, consider a **power miter saw.** This tool (also called a chopsaw or cutoff saw) is simply a circular saw mounted on a pivot assembly. It makes quick, precise crosscuts and miter cuts. Make sure you get a saw large enough to cut all the way through the stock you want to cut; a 10-inch blade handles most projects. Unless you will be doing complicated framing, there is no need to buy a model that makes compound miter cuts.

Use a **bench grinder** to sharpen tools and shape wood and metal

objects. Clamp it to your work bench, and it will be ready to use at a moment's notice.

With a good **tablesaw** you can make perfectly straight, long cuts. Use it for dado cuts as well. It also works for crosscuts and miter cuts (see page 48), but not as easily as a power miter saw. Choose a model that has a solid table that will not wiggle as you work on it, a fence that stays firmly in place, and a powerful motor. Keep in mind that you will need a good deal of room in your shop if you are going to use a tablesaw to cut sheets of plywood or long pieces of lumber.

A **radial-arm saw** is a general-purpose power saw. It makes long cuts like a tablesaw and crosscuts and miter cuts like a power miter saw. But like many multipurpose tools, it takes more time to do the job with it than with more specialized tools. Homeowners with limited space and funds, however, find this tool works quite well for a variety of cutting jobs; others prefer to buy the more specialized tools.

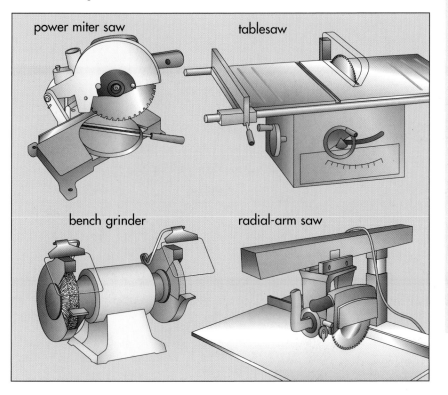

power miter saw

tablesaw

bench grinder

radial-arm saw

ORGANIZING A WORK CENTER

If you're serious about doing carpentry work around your house, you will need a convenient, comfortable, well-organized place in which to work and store the tools and materials you will accumulate. Your carpentry headquarters can be a full-fledged shop, or it may be a simple tool container and a corner set aside for lumber. But you need a work center—and the sooner, the better.

You can build your workshop in a basement, garage, seldom-used room, or even a closet or attic. A basement has several advantages. It's off the beaten path, so you needn't worry about disrupting family activities as you work. In most homes it's also one of the few areas with a sizable amount of unused space—an important factor if you want to use stationary power tools. However, if your basement tends to get wet or if it

will be difficult to get sheet goods into it, you may want to investigate other areas.

Once you've decided on the tools you would like to have, plan your space carefully. Here are some tips:

■ Make sure there is plenty of light. Large fluorescent fixtures usually work best. Make sure the lights are positioned so you won't accidentally bump the bulbs.

■ Run at least one 20-amp electrical circuit with a ground-fault circuit interrupter to the shop to provide power for your heavy-duty tools. Large shops should have separate circuits for tools and lights. Position electrical outlets strategically around the workshop so power is never far away.

■ Give yourself a way to easily carry your tools from place to place. The bucket with apron shown *below* has room for a drill,

power cord, and other large tools in the middle and smaller tools in the pockets of the apron. You may prefer a standard tool box for smaller items.

■ Have at least two sawhorses on hand (see *below* for a simple sawhorse design). Use these to support bulky sheet goods and lengths of lumber while you're working on them in the shop and to help you work at the job sites.

■ Make it as easy as possible to keep your shop clean or have a broom, dustpan, and shop vacuum on hand. For a serious shop, buy a dust collector—a central vacuuming station with tubes running to all the stationary tools. Have large garbage containers you can carry out to the trash easily.

■ If you have a forced-air furnace, make sure the dust you make cannot get sucked into it and change the filters often.

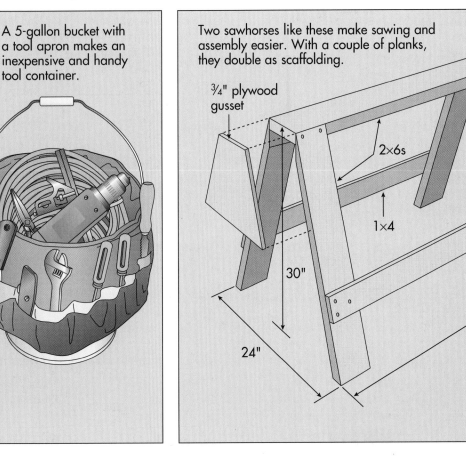

A 5-gallon bucket with a tool apron makes an inexpensive and handy tool container.

Two sawhorses like these make sawing and assembly easier. With a couple of planks, they double as scaffolding.

¾" plywood gusset

2×6s

1×4

30"

24"

42"

■ Make sure there is adequate ventilation in the work area. If possible, install an exhaust fan that can change the air in the shop every 4 minutes. The cubic feet (length times width times height) in your shop determines the size of the fan needed to do that.

■ The workbench is the activity hub of every shop. A full-size workbench typically measures 6 to 8 feet long, 24 to 36 inches deep, and 40 to 42 inches high. You may want to make it the exact height of your tablesaw or radial-arm saw. This makes it easy to handle sheets of plywood for cutting, using the bench as an additional cutting support. If you have limited space, it may make sense to have a smaller bench on wheels, so it can be stored out of the way.

The bench shown *below* can be built in a day. The plywood or hardboard top provides a smooth, hard surface and can be replaced easily when it becomes worn. The underlying planks give the bench plenty of strength and enough weight to make it a solid working surface. The bottom shelf is handy for storage. Assemble the framing with bolts, lag bolts, or screws and screw the shelf and planking in place. If you have a table-top vise, extend the front of the planking and top so it overhangs the frame by 3 inches or so and bolt the vise to the top.

■ Attach a sheet of perforated hardboard (Peg-Board) to the wall near your workbench to hang tools on. Install the board so it extends 1 or 2 inches out from the wall, so tool hooks can be inserted. If the hooks tend to pop out every time you remove a tool, glue the hooks in place with construction adhesive or hot-glue them.

■ Provide plenty of storage for your tools and materials. See page 23 for how to store lumber.

EXPERTS' INSIGHT

WORKSHOP ORGANIZERS

You need a good storage system if you want to store all your nails, screws, small tools, and various pieces of hardware so they will be easy to find. In addition to ready-made organizers, consider these possibilities:

■ Nail glass jar lids to an overhead surface, so you can reach up and unscrew jars full of fasteners or hardware. The great advantage here is that you can see what's inside each container.

■ Keep items visible. Either use open shelves or place the shelves at eye level so it's easy to find things you've stored.

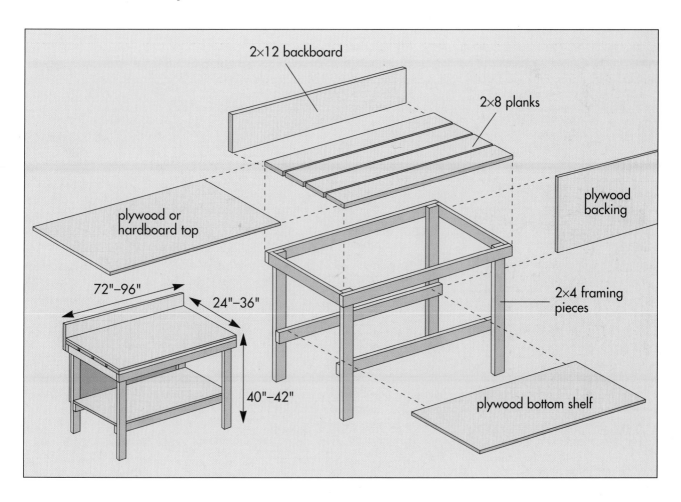

2×12 backboard

2×8 planks

plywood backing

plywood or hardboard top

72"–96"

24"–36"

40"–42"

2×4 framing pieces

plywood bottom shelf

SELECTING AND BUYING LUMBER

As you learn carpentry techniques, it's important to become familiar with the characteristics and uses of various types of lumber and how to choose the wood that will work best for a particular project.

There are two basic types of lumber—softwoods, typically made from coniferous trees, and hardwoods, made from deciduous trees. Wood is graded according to how many knots it has and the quality of its surface (see the chart below for the most common grades). Some lumberyards have their own grading systems, but they usually simply rename these standard grades.

No matter what species of lumber you buy, be on the lookout for the types of wood problems shown at *right*. A board that is heavily **twisted, bowed, cupped,** or **crooked** usually is not usable, although some bows will lie down as you nail them in place. **Knots** are only a cosmetic problem unless they are loose and likely to pop out. **Checking**, which is a rift in the surface, also is only cosmetic. **Splits** cannot be repaired and will widen in time. Cut them off.

The nominal dimensions of wood are used when ordering lumber. Keep in mind that the actual dimensions of the lumber will be less (see the chart on page 17). Large quantities of lumber are sometimes figured by the board foot. A board foot is the wood equivalent of a piece 12 nominal inches square and 1 inch thick (see chart at *bottom*). Most lumberyards will not require you to figure board feet.

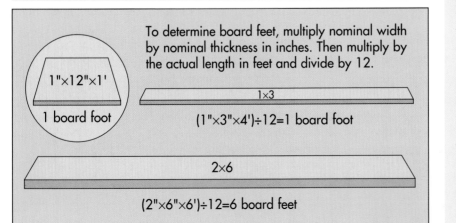

twist

bow

cup

crook

knot

check

split

SOME COMMON GRADES OF WOOD

Grades	Characteristics
Clear	Has no knots.
Select or select structural	Very high-quality wood. Broken down into Nos. 1–3 or grades A–D; the lower grades will have more knots.
No. 2 common	Has tight knots, no major blemishes; good for shelving.
No. 3 common	Some knots may be loose, often blemished or damaged.
Construction or standard	Good strength; used for general framing.
Utility	Economy grade used for rough framing.

To determine board feet, multiply nominal width by nominal thickness in inches. Then multiply by the actual length in feet and divide by 12.

1"×12"×1'
1 board foot

1×3
(1"×3"×4')÷12=1 board foot

2×6
(2"×6"×6')÷12=6 board feet

LUMBER SELECTOR

Type	Description and Uses	Nominal Sizes	Actual Sizes
Furring	Rough wood of small dimensions. For furring drywall and paneling, interior and exterior trim, shimming, stakes, crates, light-duty frames, latticework, and edging.	1×2 1×3	$3/4$×$1\,1/2$ $3/4$×$2\,1/2$
Finish lumber	Smooth-finished lumber. For paneling, trim, shelving, light framing, structural finishing, forming, siding, decking, casing, valances, cabinets, built-ins, and furniture.	1×4 1×6 1×8 1×10 1×12	$3/4$×$3\,1/2$ $3/4$×$5\,1/2$ $3/4$×$7\,1/4$ $3/4$×$9\,1/4$ $3/4$×$11\,1/4$
Tongue-and-groove	Tongues and grooves fit into each other for a tight fit. For decorative interior wall treatments, exterior siding, flooring, and subflooring.	1×4 1×6 1×8	Actual sizes vary from mill to mill
Shiplap	One edge fits on top of the other. For decorative wall treatments, siding, decking, exterior sheathing, subflooring, and roof sheathing.	1×4 1×6 1×8	$3/4$×$3\,1/8$ $3/4$×$5\,1/8$ $3/4$×$6\,7/8$
Dimensional lumber	Studs are usually 2×4, sometimes 2×6. "Planks" are 6 or more inches wide. For structural framing (wall studs, ceiling and floor joists, rafters, headers, top and bottom plates), structural finishing, forming, exterior decking and fencing, and stair components (stringers, steps).	2×2 2×3 2×4 2×6 2×8 2×10 2×12 4×4 4×6 6×6	$1\,1/2$×$1\,1/2$ $1\,1/2$×$2\,1/2$ $1\,1/2$×$3\,1/2$ $1\,1/2$×$5\,1/2$ $1\,1/2$×$7\,1/4$ $1\,1/2$×$9\,1/4$ $1\,1/2$×$11\,1/4$ $3\,1/2$×$3\,1/2$ $3\,1/2$×$5\,1/2$ $5\,1/2$×$5\,1/2$
Glue-laminate	Layers of dimensional lumber laid flat on top of each other and laminated into one solid piece. Used for rafters, joists, and beams. Can be stained for exposed beams.	4×10 4×12 6×10 6×12	$3\,1/2$×9 $3\,1/2$×12 $5\,1/2$×9 $5\,1/2$×12
Micro-laminate	Veneers glued together with crossing grains like plywood, only thicker. For rafters, joists, and beams.	4×12	$3\,1/2$×$11\,3/8$

SELECTING SOFTWOODS

Unless you're installing major structural components, such as floor or ceiling joists, that will bear significant weight, you can't make a serious mistake when buying softwoods. In most cases, you simply want to buy the wood that looks best or is the least-expensive alternative.

Softwood usually is less expensive than hardwood (see page 19) because it comes from trees that grow faster. In general, the disadvantage of softwood is evident in its name; it actually is soft. If you use softwood for furniture and other objects that will get handled and bumped against, plan on applying a hard finish or paint. Even then, it will not be as durable as hardwood.

Most retail suppliers stock only a few species of softwood. The chart below summarizes the chief characteristics of each. In most cases, you won't be choosing between species, but between grades of lumber. Which grade you choose depends on the nature of your project.

Softwood grading is tricky because several grading systems exist. Most often, however, you'll find two general classifications: select and common.

Use select lumber, which comes in several subgrades, for trim or cabinetry where finished appearance counts. For all other projects, common lumber will do nicely. Common lumber is graded as No. 1, No. 2, and No. 3.

With some suppliers, you can dispense with the grades and talk about more straightforward categories, such as "clear" (without knots) and "tight-knot" (having only small knots without cracks).

Of course, the better the grade—that is, the fewer the defects—the more you pay for the product. Often, however, a better grade is only slightly more expensive. Once you gain some experience, if you sort through the lumber rack carefully, you often can find pieces that are out of their class—for instance, a piece of No. 2 common that actually could have been classified as select.

SOFTWOOD SELECTOR

Species	Characteristics	Common Uses
Cedar, cypress	Similar to redwood—only the darker wood is rot-resistant. Weak, brittle; resists warping; pleasant aroma; easy to cut.	Siding, paneling, rough trim, roof shingles and shakes, decks.
Fir, larch	Heavy, very strong, hard; holds nails well; good resistance to warping and shrinkage; somewhat difficult to cut.	Framing studs, joists, posts, and beams; flooring; subflooring.
"Hem/fir"	A general classification that takes in a variety of species. Lightweight, soft, fairly strong; warps easily; may shrink; easy to cut.	Framing, exterior fascia, flooring, subflooring, trim.
Pine	From eastern, northern, and western trees. Very light, soft, fairly weak,; good resistance to warping, but with a tendency to shrink; easy to cut.	Paneling, trim (molding), flooring, cabinets.
Redwood	Durable and resistant to rot and insects if you get the darker-colored heartwood. Light, soft, not as strong as fir or Southern pine; tendency to split; easy to cut.	Exterior posts and beams, siding, paneling, decks, fences.
Southern pine	Very hard, stiff, excellent strength; holds nails well; has a tendency to crack, splinter, warp; cuts with average ease.	Framing, subflooring.
Spruce	Lightweight, soft, fairly strong; resistant to splitting and warping; easy to work.	Framing, flooring, subflooring, trim (molding).
Treated lumber	Several species can be treated—most often, fir, "hem/fir," and Southern pine are used. Green or brown color will fade in time, leaving the wood a dirty gray; extremely resistant to rot and insects.	Bottom framing plates that rest on concrete; other framing that might come into contact with water, decks, fences.

SELECTING HARDWOODS

You can buy various types of plastic-laminated products made to look like hardwood, but there is no substitute for the real thing. Hardwood flooring and trim give a home an elegance unmatched by any other product. For furniture and cabinetry, nothing quite measures up in appearance and durability.

Unfortunately, hardwood trees grow slowly, so prices tend to be higher than for softwood. But prices fluctuate widely from year to year, and often the difference is surprisingly small. Oak flooring, for example, is sometimes cheaper than softwood flooring.

The more expensive hardwoods are milled to make use of virtually every splinter of wood. Instead of the standard sizes, some hardwoods are sold in pieces of varying lengths and widths. Sometimes the boards are smooth-surfaced only on two sides (S2S), leaving the edges rough. Hardwoods may be priced by the board foot (see page 16).

Hardwood grading differs from that of softwoods. It is based primarily on the amount of clear surface area on the board. The best grade is FAS (firsts and seconds), which is the most knot-free. Select boards have defects on one side only: No. 1 Common has tiny, tight knots; No. 2 Common has larger knots.

Most lumberyards and home centers can't afford to maintain an extensive inventory of hardwood lumber and generally stock only a limited assortment of a few species. For the best selection, find a store that specializes in hardwoods. They stock or can order a wide selection of species.

HARDWOOD SELECTOR

Species	Characteristics	Common Uses
Birch	Hard, strong; fine-grained; resists shrinking and warping. Similar in color to maple—sometimes used as a cheaper replacement. Finishes fairly well; hard to cut.	Paintable cabinets, paneling, furniture.
Mahogany	Durable; fine-grained; resistant to shrinking, warping, and swelling. Finishes well; easy to cut. (Not to be confused with luan mahogany, a much cheaper material that is used for veneers and plywoods.)	Fine furniture, cabinets, millwork, veneers.
Maple	Extremely hard, strong; pieces with bird's-eye or wavy grains are highly prized. Color ranges from reddish to nearly white in color. Finishes well; difficult to cut.	Flooring (basketball and bowling alley floors are made of maple), butcher blocks, veneers, millwork, and molding.
Poplar	Lightweight, soft for a hardwood; fine-grained. White to yellow-brown in color. Paints well; easy to cut.	Paintable furniture, cabinets, trim, places where a less-expensive hardwood will do.
Red oak	Hard, strong, rigid; pronounced open grain; resists warping, but may shrink if not well dried. Reddish color. Finishes well; moderately hard to cut.	Flooring, furniture, cabinets, molding, stair rails.
Walnut	Hard, heavy, extra strong; fairly pronounced, straight grain; resists warping and shrinking. Light to dark brown in color. Finishes well; cuts fairly easily.	Fine furniture and cabinets, millwork, paneling, inlays, veneers.
White oak	Hard, strong; open-grained, but not as pronounced as red oak; resists shrinking and warping. Golden color. Finishes well; moderately hard to cut.	Better than red oak for flooring—less variation in color. Millwork, molding, furniture, cabinets, stair rails, balusters.

SELECTING SHEET GOODS

Sheet goods are easy to work with and an inexpensive way to neatly cover large surface areas. For many applications, they provide the strength and appearance you need at a fraction of the cost of dimensional lumber.

Plywood is made by laminating thin layers (or plies) of wood to each other using water-resistant glue. The plies are sandwiched with the grain of each successive ply running at 90 degrees to the grain of the previous layer. This gives plywood its tremendous strength, as you will find if you try to break a piece in two. The front and back surface plies may be made of softwood, usually fir, or hardwood. A plywood face surface rated "A" is smooth and free of defects; "B," "C," and "D" faces are progressively rougher. Both faces need not be graded the same, for example, "A-C." T–111 plywood siding is made with exterior adhesive and a rough veneer.

Wood particles, sawdust, and glue are compressed and bonded together by heat to form **particleboard** and **hardboard**. This process produces a material that is hard, but easy to break. Hardboard comes in tempered (very hard) and untempered (softer) composition and is available in a variety of textures. Particleboard also comes in a variety of densities. Particleboard laminated with a plastic surface is handy for cabinet construction. **Waferboard** is made by a similar process, but with scraps of thin wood rather than sawdust, making it similar to plywood.

Drywall, sometimes called wallboard, is made of gypsum powder sandwiched between layers of heavy paper. **Cement board** is made with crushed rock and a nylon mesh.

SHEET GOODS SELECTOR

Material	Grades and Common Types	Thickness (in inches)	Common Panel Sizes (in feet)	Typical Uses
Plywood sheathing	C-D, C-D Exterior	3/8, 1/2, 5/8, 3/4	4×8	Sheathing, subflooring, underlayment, structural supports. Tongue-and-groove and shiplap versions are available.
Finish plywood	A-B, A-C, B-C	1/4, 3/8, 1/2, 5/8, 3/4	4×8, 2×4	Cabinets, cabinet doors, shelves, soffits.
Hardwood plywood	A-A (or A-2), G1S (good one side); hardwood side sometimes labeled N	1/4, 3/4	4×8, 2×4	Cabinets, cabinet doors, shelves, wall panels.
Luan subflooring	Only one type	1/4	4×8, 2×4	Underlayment for vinyl tiles or sheet goods, backing for cabinets.
T-111 siding	Rough, with grooves variously spaced	3/8, 1/2, 5/8	4×8, 4×9	Exterior siding.
Waferboard	Only one type	1/4, 7/16, 1/2, 3/4	4×8	Roof sheathing, underlayment.
Particleboard	Density of material varies	1/4, 3/8, 1/2, 5/8, 3/4	4×8, 2×4	Underlayment, core material for laminated furniture and countertops.
Hardboard	Standard, tempered, perforated	1/8, 1/4	4×8, 2×4	Underlayment, drawer bottoms and partitions, cabinet backs, perforated tool organizers.
Drywall	Standard, greenboard (water-resistant)	3/8, 1/2, 5/8	4×8, 4×10, 4×12	Interior walls.
Cement board	Only one type	5/16, 1/2	32"×60"	Backing for wall tiles, underlayment for ceramic floors.

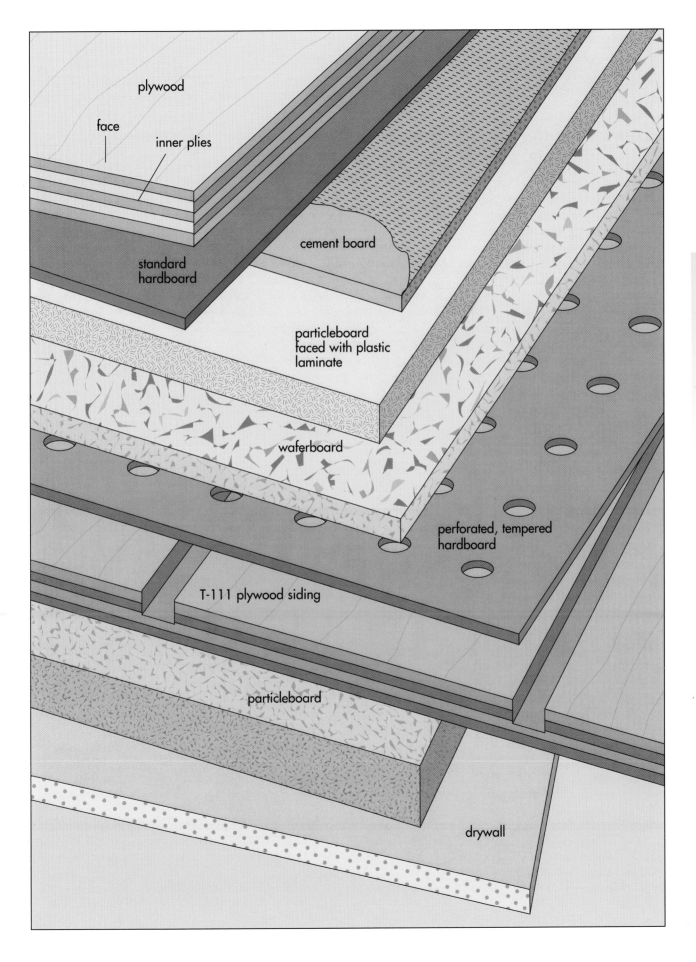

plywood

face

inner plies

standard
hardboard

cement board

particleboard
faced with plastic
laminate

waferboard

perforated, tempered
hardboard

T-111 plywood siding

particleboard

drywall

SELECTING AND ORDERING MOLDING

All rooms use at least some molding, usually along the base of walls and around windows and doors. In those places, molding covers up gaps. Other molding protects corners from dents or protects walls from damage by chair backs. In other places, such as around mantels, along the ceiling, and where paint and wall coverings meet in the middle of a wall, molding serves a decorative function. The molding you choose goes a long way toward defining the look of a room, whether it's minimalist or lushly decorative.

Molding is available in random lengths from 6 to 16 feet. Most is made of softwood, usually pine. Some popular types are available in hardwood, usually oak. These are a little more expensive.

The cost of molding does add up, so make a list of each piece you need, rounding the length up to the nearest foot, then add 5 percent to allow for trimming and fitting. See pages 72–75 for molding installation tips.

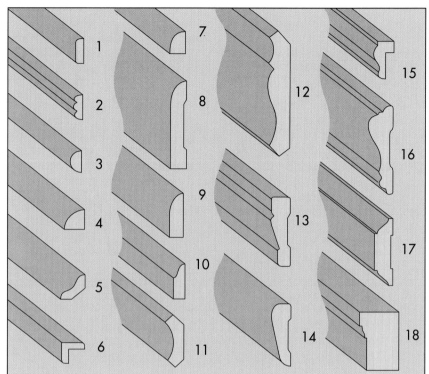

Money $ Saver

ALTERNATIVE MATERIALS

■ Finger-jointed molding is made of short pieces joined end to end. It costs less than regular molding, but you may need to sand the joints smooth.
■ Plastic molding is inexpensive, but has wood-grain finishes that may not suit your style. (Some can be painted.)
■ If you plan to paint molding rather than stain it, you may be able to save time and money with a preprimed molding.
■ Paper-covered hardboard molding also costs less, but can be difficult to cut neatly and the paper may tear later.

MOLDING SELECTOR

Common Types	Typical Uses
Screen bead; regular (1) and fluted (2)	Both cover seams where screening fastens to frames; finish edges of shelves.
Half round (3)	Serves as screen bead, shelf edging, and lattice.
Quarter round (4)	Serves as base shoe and inside corner guard.
Inside corner (5) and outside corner (6)	Both conceal seams and protect areas where walls meet at corners.
Base shoe (7) and baseboard (8)	Both trim and protect walls at their base.
Stop; ranch (9) and colonial (10)	Both attach to door jambs to limit door swing; hold inside sash of windows in place.
Cove (11) and crown (12)	Both trim and conceal joint between walls and ceilings.
Casing; colonial (13) and ranch (14)	Both trim around interior windows and doors.
Plycap (15)	Conceals plywood edge; tops off wainscoting.
Chair rail (16)	Protects walls from chair backs; hides seams where wall materials meet.
Batten (17)	Conceals vertical and horizontal panel seams.
Brick mold (18)	Used with all types of exterior cladding (not just brick) to trim around doors and windows.

HANDLING AND STORING MATERIALS

One of the joys of having your own shop is the pile of useful materials you collect over time. To ensure a safe, uneventful trip home from your home center, secure materials to your vehicle with rope, bungee cords, or twine. For large purchases or if your vehicle cannot handle the load, pay a little extra and have the materials delivered to your house.

When transporting or unloading sheet goods, have a helper on hand. If that's not possible, lift a panel with one hand near the center of each long edge, as shown in the inset *below*. Pick it up and rest it on your shoulder; avoid carrying it with a bent back. The

exception is drywall; because it's thin, heavy, and brittle, it can snap under its own weight. Get help with drywall. Take care not to damage the edges or scratch the surface of the sheets.

Too quickly, however, your pile of material can become a headache and an eyesore. To keep boards and sheet goods easily accessible and prevent warping and other damage, keep these tips in mind:

■ Store materials in a cool, dry place, off the floor. Moisture can distort lumber, delaminate some plywoods, and render drywall useless. If your basement gets wet occasionally, store materials above the high-water line.

■ Ideally, sheet goods should be stored flat. Because most people don't have room to do this, it's best to stand sheet goods on edge, as shown *below*, as vertical as possible to keep them from bowing.

■ Build a storage rack like the one shown *below* to keep lumber at eye level. You want to see the ends of boards clearly and be able to pull out what you need easily.

■ If you don't build a rack, store lumber flat and weight it down at each end and in the center to prevent warping and other distortions. Weighting is especially important if the wood has a high moisture content.

1×3

1×4

Pick up sheet goods by lifting from knees, not back..

Keep materials off floor; add height if moisture is likely.

SELECTING NAILS

Many types and sizes of nails are available, each one engineered for a specific use. The differences may seem small, but they can have a significant effect on the soundness and appearance of your job. Here's a guide to choosing among the standard types of nails:

Use **common** nails and **box** nails for framing jobs. Box nails are a bit thinner for lighter work. **Cement-coated** nails drive in more easily and hold more firmly. Use **roofing** nails for roof shingles and wherever a wide head is needed to hold material that might tear if a smaller head is used. Choose hot-dipped over electroplated **galvanized** nails; they'll last much longer.

Casing and **finishing** nails handle medium- and heavy-duty finishing work. For very fine work, use **wire brads. Ring-shank** and **spiral** nails grab wood more tightly than conventional nails. Specially hardened **masonry** nails penetrate mortar joints, brick, and even concrete. **Corrugated fasteners** are used mainly for strengthening wood joints; they do not hold well by themselves.

You can save money by buying nails in bulk, rather than in the box. However, it is handy to have boxes marked with the nail size.

MEASUREMENTS

PENNIES AND INCHES

In Great Britain in the 1400s, you could buy 100 medium-size nails for 8 pennies. It didn't take long for inflation to destroy that designation, but we use the term penny to this day to size nails. The abbreviation "d" for penny is derived from *denarius,* a small, silver Roman coin used in Britain that, from early times, equated with a penny.

Inch equivalent of nails sizes:
3d=1¼"	10d=3"
4d=1½"	12d=3¼"
6d=2"	16d=3½"
7d=2¼"	20d=4"
8d=2½"	

THE NAIL FOR THE JOB

Use nails three times as long as the thickness of the material you are fastening. For instance, to attach a 1×4 (¾ inch thick), a 6-penny nail (2 inches long) will be a bit short. An 8-penny nail (2½ inches long, a little more than three times the thickness of the 1×4) will do better. Make sure the nail will not poke through the material to which you are fastening.

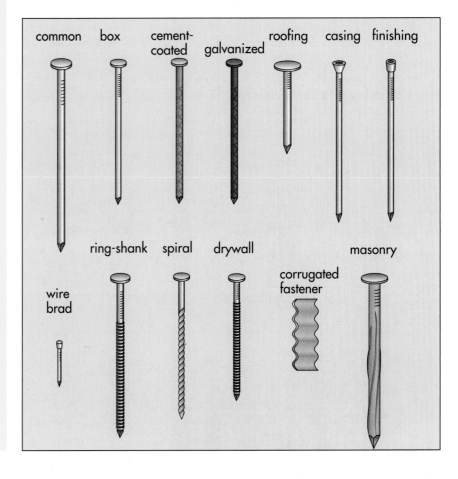

SELECTING SCREWS AND BOLTS

For the few seconds they take to drive in, nails do a remarkable holding job. Yet for the little extra time it takes to drive in a screw, you get a tighter-holding fastener, a neater appearance, and another plus—ease of disassembly. In fact, drywall screws teamed with cordless electric drills have created a mini-revolution in fasteners, including everything from deck screws to general-purpose wood screws.

The most common slot configurations for screws are the **slotted head** and the **Phillips head**, which has an X-shaped slot. **Square-drive** screws are more rare, but are growing in popularity.

There are three head shapes from which to choose. A **flathead** screw can be driven flush with or slightly below the surface of the wood. Use **ovalhead** screws with trim washers for a finished appearance. Install **roundhead** screws when you want the screw head to show.

General-purpose or **drywall** screws offer an inexpensive and easy way to fasten items together. You can buy them by the pound, and they drive easily using a drill with a screwdriver bit. **Trim head** screws use a smaller Phillips or square-drive bit. They hold better than finish nails, but the countersink hole will be larger.

Use **masonry** screws (often referred to by the brand name Tap-Con) to fasten material to masonry or concrete surfaces. Simply drill the correct-size hole in the masonry surface and drive in the screw. Drive a **hanger** screw into a ceiling joist and fasten the object to be hung using the nut and thread on its lower half.

Use **lag** screws for heavy-duty fastening. Drill a pilot hole and drive in the screw with a wrench.

As with nails, screws should be three times as long as the thickness of the board being fastened. When buying screws, specify the gauge (diameter) you want. The thicker the gauge, the greater its holding power. Make sure you have the correct-size drill bit if drilling pilot holes (see the box at right). For more on driving in screws, see pages 54–55.

Machine bolts have a head that can be turned with a wrench. **Carriage bolts** have round heads for a finished appearance. When buying bolts, be sure to get the correct gauge and length; it must be longer than the materials you are fastening, so you can add the nut and washers. (For more on fastening with bolts, see page 56.) Thin metal can be joined with self-tapping **sheet-metal screws**.

ADHESIVES

Many carpentry jobs call for adhesives, either as the primary or secondary fastener. Purchase a supply of wood glue for general-purpose work, construction adhesive in tubes, two-part epoxy glue for extra-strong holding, panel adhesive for installing drywall or paneling, and perhaps a hot-glue gun with glue sticks.

EXPERTS' INSIGHT

DRILLING PILOT HOLES

To see if a drill bit is the correct size to make your pilot hole, grip both bit and screw together with your fingers. The bit should be slightly thinner than the width of the screw threads.

The thickness of a pilot hole can vary depending on the wood. With softwoods, you can use a smaller hole than you would with hardwoods. Always drill a test hole and make sure the screw will hold tight before you proceed to drill a number of holes in the finished material.

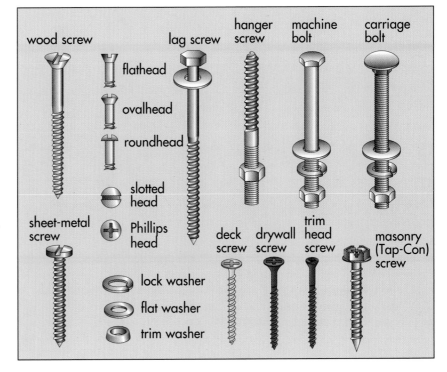

SELECTING HARDWARE

The items shown on these two pages represent just a few of the options available in specialized hardware. At your hardware store or home center, you'll find a product designed for almost every conceivable carpentry need.

When you want to strengthen a weak wood joint, reach for a metal plate or brace, as shown *below left.* **Mending plates** reinforce end-to-end joints; **T-plates** handle end-to-edge joints. **Flat corner irons** strengthen corner joints by attaching to the face of the material; **angle brackets** do the same thing, but attach to the inside or outside edges.

Shelf standards, as shown *below right,* come in a variety of configurations and finishes suitable for utility or more decorative uses. Most standards can be installed on the wall or into supports behind the shelves. Some standards can be installed on either side of the shelves. **Adjustable standards and brackets** come in a variety of colors, sizes, and finishes. Use **utility brackets** for nonadjustable shelving in places where appearance is not important. **Closet rod brackets** let you attach a shelf and a closet rod to the same piece of hardware.

There is a large choice of door and cabinet hardware, as shown on *page 27.* Most full-size doors hang on the classic **butt hinge** (see page 88). **Piano hinges** mount flush on cabinets and chests, combining great strength with a slim, finished look. **Strap hinges** and **T-hinges** often are used on gates and trunk lids.

There are four basic types of cabinet hinges. **Decorative hinges** work only for doors that are flush with the frame. Use **front- or side-mount offset hinges** for doors that are either flush with the frame or that have lips that overlay the frame. If a door completely overlays the frame, use a **pivot hinge** or a self-closing **European-style hidden hinge.** To open your cabinet doors, fit them with **knobs** or **pulls,** available in a myriad of sizes and styles. **Friction, roller, bullet,** or **magnetic catches** keep cabinet doors closed. (If you are using self-closing hinges, these catches aren't necessary.)

For smooth-operating drawers, choose side-mounted **drawer slides** like the one shown on *page 27.* For extra household security, add a **chain lock** to your door.

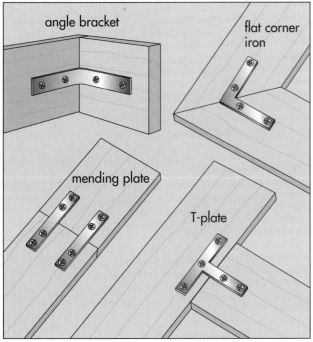

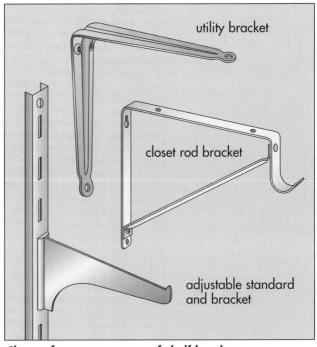

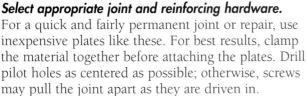

Select appropriate joint and reinforcing hardware.
For a quick and fairly permanent joint or repair, use inexpensive plates like these. For best results, clamp the material together before attaching the plates. Drill pilot holes as centered as possible; otherwise, screws may pull the joint apart as they are driven in.

Choose from many types of shelf brackets.
If you've ever tried to make a shelf bracket out of lumber, you'll know how much time and effort is saved by these handy pieces of hardware. For more on installing shelf hardware and shelf construction, see pages 82–85.

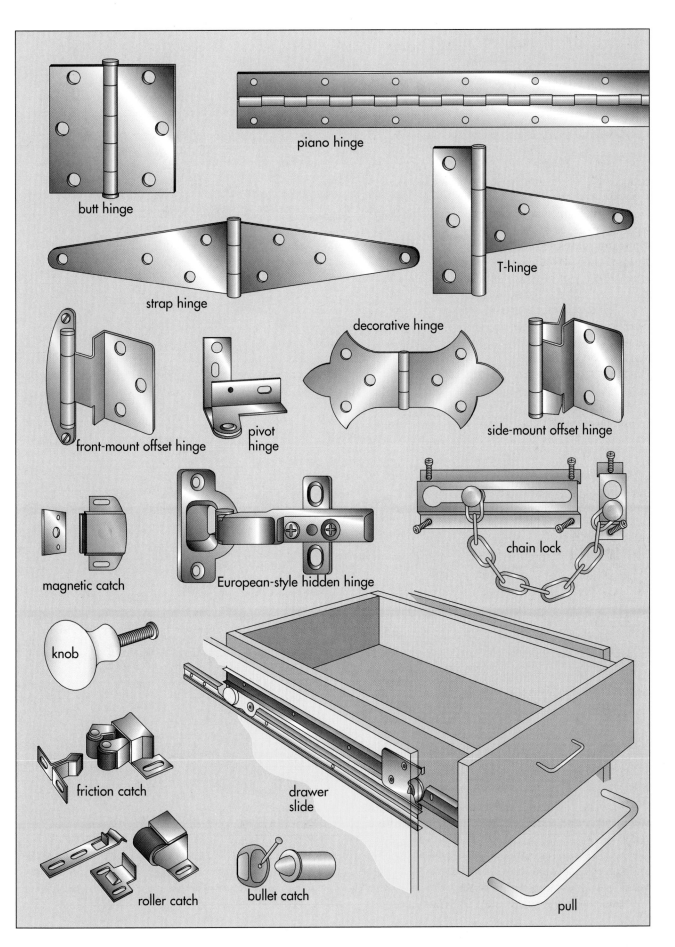

butt hinge

piano hinge

T-hinge

strap hinge

decorative hinge

front-mount offset hinge

pivot hinge

side-mount offset hinge

magnetic catch

European-style hidden hinge

chain lock

knob

friction catch

drawer slide

roller catch

bullet catch

pull

MEASURING AND MARKING

Accurate measuring and marking are the bases of successful carpentry. A mistake in measuring often means wasted time and material. Though it may seem simple, good measuring technique does not come naturally. It takes practice.

Don't rush your measuring. Take your time and double-check your work. Adopt the carpenters' maxim, "Measure twice, cut once."

No matter what measuring device you use, get comfortable with it and learn how to read it accurately. Many a board has met its ruin because someone couldn't distinguish a ¼-inch mark from a ⅛-inch mark. Once you've made a measurement, don't trust your memory. Jot down the figure on a piece of paper or a wood scrap.

Marking, not reading, the measurement is the difficulty. Make a clear mark (see page 29) using a sharp No. 2 pencil, the thin edge of a sharpened carpenter's pencil, a knife, or a scratch awl (especially if working with sheet metal).

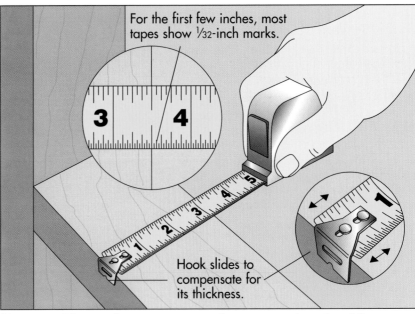

Measure with a steel tape.
A steel tape is the most popular measuring device because it does most jobs with ease. Note that the hook at the end of the tape slides back and forth slightly to compensate for its own thickness. This means that whether you hook the tape on a board end for an outside measurement or push it against a surface for an inside measurement, the result will be accurate. For the first few inches of most tapes, each inch is divided into ¹⁄₃₂-inch increments to facilitate extra-fine measurements.

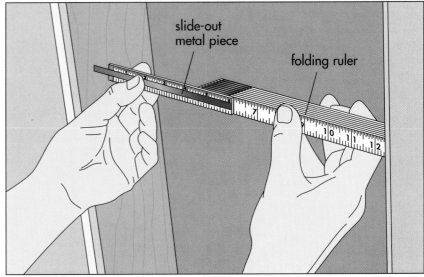

Take an inside measurement.
Where outside measurement is difficult (here the drywall is in the way of measuring between the outside edges of the 2×4s) make an inside-to-inside measurement. A folding ruler with a slide-out metal piece works best. Extend it, measure, and hold the slide with your thumb until the measurement is transferred. You can use a tape measure for such measurements, but it is difficult to be accurate because you have to add an amount to compensate for the length of the tape body.

Make a V mark, not a line.

Marking with a simple line often leads to inaccuracies. By the time you're ready to saw, it's easy to forget which end of the line marks the spot—or where to cut on a thick line from a blunt pencil. For greater accuracy, mark your measurements with a V so you know precisely where to strike the cut line. To ensure pinpoint accuracy, place the point of your pencil at the V, slide the square to it, then make your line.

If you need to extend cut lines across several boards, use a framing square. For longer lines, use a drywall square.

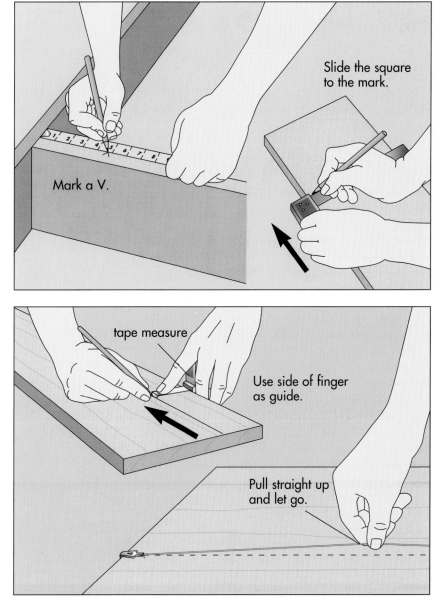

Slide the square to the mark.

Mark a V.

Mark for rip cuts.

Need to mark a cutoff line along the length of a board or a piece of plywood? If the line is parallel to the edge of the board and accuracy isn't critical, use your tape measure as a scribing device. Hold your tape so that a pencil laid against its end will make the correct line. Hold the tape and pencil firmly and pull evenly toward you, letting the tape body or your thumbnail slide along the board edge. For sheet goods, first mark the cutoff line at both ends, then snap a chalk line between the two marks, or clamp a straightedge in place and draw a mark.

tape measure

Use side of finger as guide.

Pull straight up and let go.

Allow for the saw kerf.

When you cut material, the saw blade reduces some of it to sawdust. So, when measuring, you must allow for the narrow opening left in the blade's wake—called the kerf. Usually, a kerf is about $\frac{1}{8}$ inch wide. If you're making just one cut, account for the kerf by marking the waste side of the cutoff line with an X. There's no confusion then as to the side of the line on which to cut.

If you are cutting multiple pieces out of the same piece of lumber, make double marks to allow for the kerf. Otherwise, you will cut each piece too short.

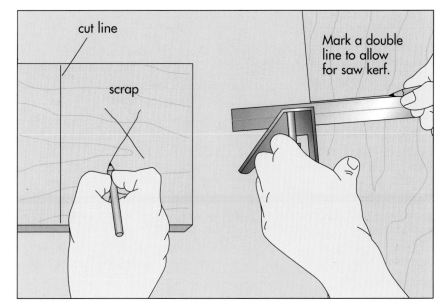

cut line

scrap

Mark a double line to allow for saw kerf.

HOLDING AND MEASURING IN PLACE

The most accurate and mistake-proof way of measuring is not to use a measuring device at all. Simply hold a piece where it needs to fit and mark it. You can do this for a simple cutoff. At other times, such as when you need to cut a board in two directions, use a combination of techniques: Hold and mark, then measure. Often this method isn't feasible, especially where access is limited or when the lumber being cut is too bulky to be held in place. But take advantage of this foolproof approach when you can.

YOU'LL NEED

TIME: Less than a minute for most measurements.
SKILLS: A steady hand and a good eye for accurate marking.
TOOLS: Pencil, speed square.

Hold this end as far out as possible—it should just barely touch the board.

Hold and mark for a cutoff.
When you need to cut a board to length, begin by checking one end of the board for square. Press the square-cut end against one side of the opening, and mark the other end for cutting. To avoid distorting the measurement, don't push the square-cut end into the space any more than needed.

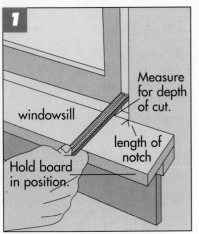

1. To mark for a cutout, first measure the depth of the cut.
When you need to cut a board in two or three directions to make it fit around something, begin by holding the board in place. Make a small mark showing where the cutout is to be cut to length. Then measure how deep the cutout must be by measuring the distance between the leading edge of the board and the place where it must end up once it's cut.

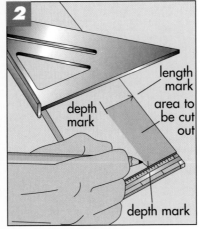

2. Transfer measurement mark.
Use a square to extend the length mark. With a tape measure, transfer the depth measurement to two places on the board—at the length mark and at the end of the cutout. Use a square to draw a line from the length mark to the depth mark. With a straightedge, mark a line between the two depth marks.

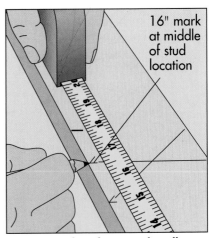

16" mark at middle of stud location

Lay out a plate for a stud wall.
When building a wall, the studs (upright 2×4s) must be 16 inches on center; that is, you want 48- or 96-inch drywall or paneling sheets to end in the middle of a stud. To make marks for studs, mark every 16 inches, minus ¾ inch (15¼ inches, 31¼ inches, and so on). Measure over 1½ inches and make another mark. Draw lines at your marks and an X between to show stud location (see page 91).

SQUARING, PLUMBING, AND LEVELING

Most carpentry projects—from making simple shelves to building walls—require that you square the work. Check for square at every stage of your work: corners, uprights, and board ends.

Making sure that work is plumb and level is equally important. Walls, cabinets, doors—nearly every permanent installation—must be plumb (perpendicular to the earth) and level (parallel to the earth). Don't assume existing walls or floors are square, level, or plumb. Most often they are not because of imperfect construction or settling that has taken place over the years. Techniques shown in this section will help you keep your carpentry projects straight and true.

TIME: A couple of minutes or less to check that work is square, plumb, or level.
SKILLS: Use of squares and levels.
TOOLS: Combination, speed, framing squares; 2- or 4-foot level; other levels.

TOOLS TO USE

THE MULTIPURPOSE SPEED SQUARE

Almost every carpenter's belt contains a hammer, utility knife, pencil, and the ever-handy speed square. With a speed square, you can quickly mark 45- and 90-degree angles simply by holding the square with its body firmly against a factory edge. Other angles are marked on the body of the square and can be used with a fair degree of accuracy. In addition, the speed square is handy as a guide for cutting square corners (see page 37).

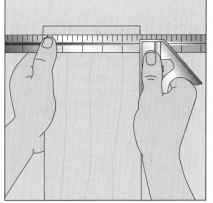

Check board ends for square.
All your careful measuring will be wasted if you start with a piece of lumber that is not square—one edge will be longer than the other. Check the board end by holding a combination square with the body or handle firmly against a factory edge. If the end isn't square, mark a square line and trim the board.

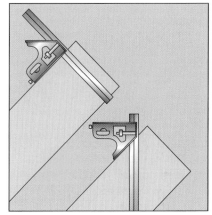

Use a combination square.
With this tool you can easily check for either 45- or 90-degree angles. Also, by sliding the blade, you can check depths. This tool can go out of square if it is dropped, so check it once in a while against a square factory edge (such as the corner of a sheet of plywood).

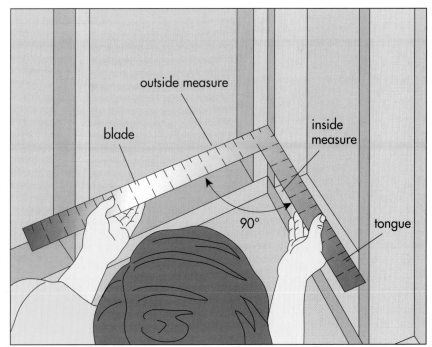

Use a framing square.
For larger jobs, use a framing square. Lay the square up against two members where they meet. If the tongue and the blade of the square rest neatly against the members, the sides are perpendicular. Or, place the square on the outside. Again, if the square touches the members at all points, the unit is square. When using a framing square for measuring, be sure to read the correct scale—inside or outside.

TOOLS TO USE

DRYWALL SQUARE

This tool, sometimes called a T-square, helps you cut drywall much faster than other tools. It is well worth its price if you need to cut a lot of drywall. It also is useful for measuring and marking other sheet goods, particularly plywood and particleboard. Because the blade is a full 4 feet long, you need make only one mark rather than two when marking for a cutoff, and you don't have to align straightedges or mess with chalk lines. A drywall square can get out of square if you're not careful with it. Take care to rest it in places where it won't get banged around. Periodically test it for square by holding it against two factory edges of a sheet of drywall or plywood.

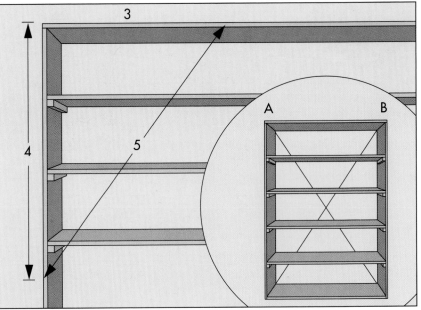

Use the 3-4-5 method.
For large projects, test if a corner is square by using geometry. You don't need to remember the Pythagorean theorem. Just remember "3-4-5." On one side, mark a point 3 feet from the corner. On the other side, mark a point 4 feet from the corner. If the distance between the two marks is exactly 5 feet, it is square. For extra large projects, use multiples such as 6-8-10 or 9-12-15.

As a double check, measure the length of the diagonals. If the project is square, the distance between two opposite corners (marked A in the drawing *above*) will equal the distance between the other two corners (B).

Check for plumb.
To see if a piece is perfectly vertical—plumb—hold a level against one face of the vertical surface and look at the air bubble in the level's lower glass vial. If it rests between the two guide marks, the piece is plumb.

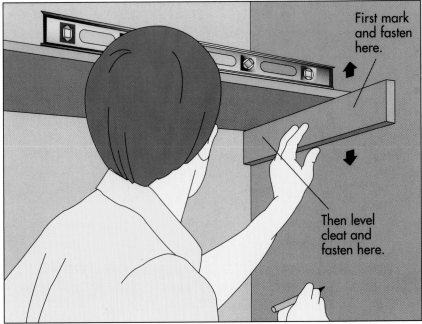

First mark and fasten here.

Then level cleat and fasten here.

Check for level.
In most cases, you can simply set your carpenter's level atop the piece to see if it's level. Raise or lower the piece until the bubble rests between the marks. Mark the position of the piece and remove the level (you don't want to risk knocking it to the floor). Add a fastener to the cleat near the level mark, level the cleat, and finish fastening.

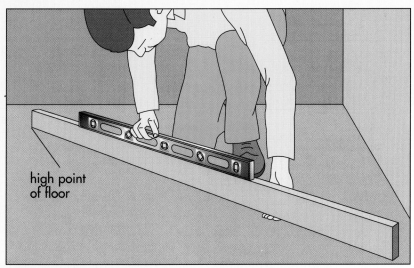

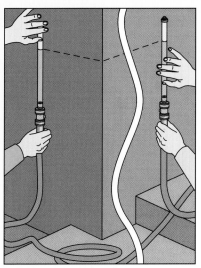

To test for level over long distances, use a board ...

If you need to see if an entire floor is level, select a long, straight board. (Sight down its length to see that it's not bowed.) Place a carpenter's level in the center of the board and raise one end or the other until the bubble is centered between the two lines. Slide the board around until you are sure you have found the high point of the floor. Level the board from this high point and measure the distance from the floor to the bottom of the raised end of the board to see how far out of level the floor is.

or use a water level.

This tool enables you to quickly check for level in awkward situations or over long distances. Basically a long hose and two transparent tubes filled with water, this tool works on the principle that water seeks its own level. Mark at water level.

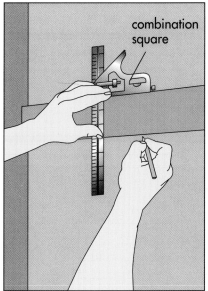

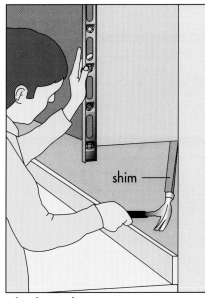

Use small levels in tight spots.

In places where you can't fit in a carpenter's level, use the level that comes on some combination squares or a torpedo level (a short version of a carpenter's level). Or, if you know that an adjoining member or wall is plumb, measure to see that the piece is square to it.

Plumb a cabinet.

When installing cabinets, make sure they are plumb in both directions or the doors will shut or open by themselves. With the cabinet fastened to the wall loosely, hold a level against a vertical framing piece. Tap in shims until the bubble indicates that the cabinet is plumb.

EXPERTS' INSIGHT

TEST YOUR LEVEL

■ Test a new level for accuracy before buying it. If the first one you try isn't accurate, the next one on the shelf may be. If you own a level, test it to see if it has been knocked out of alignment.

■ To make sure your level is accurate, set it on a shelf or table and note the location of the bubble. Then, turn the level around end-for-end on the same surface. It should give exactly the same reading.

■ If it is not accurate, you may be able to adjust it by loosening the four small screws holding the bubble assembly and turning the assembly until it is correct. If the level isn't adjustable, you'll have to buy a new one.

USING SPECIAL MARKING TECHNIQUES

A flexible steel tape measure, a square, and a level usually will equip you to mark your lumber for cutting. But sometimes you'll come across a situation where you'll have to mark around the irregular contours of molding, brick, or stone; mark curved shapes; or mark for angles other than 45 degrees and 90 degrees. These aren't challenges to be left only to master carpenters. The simple techniques in this section are for marking unusual shapes.

EXPERTS' INSIGHT

MAKING AND USING TEMPLATES

■ For material in which you are making multiple or complicated cuts, make a template or pattern before you make the cut. Often, the piece of lumber or sheet goods you are replacing can serve as the template. Carefully remove the old piece, take out any nails or screws that are in it, place it over the new lumber, and trace its outline.

■ At other times, you may need to make a template. Cut a piece of stiff cardboard with a knife or make a pattern out of a piece of scrap wood. Experiment until the template fits exactly, but don't experiment on your final, expensive materials.

■ Whenever you use a template, be sure that it does not slide around as you make your marks—you may need to clamp or tack it in place. Watch your pencil line carefully to see that it is tight against the template at all points.

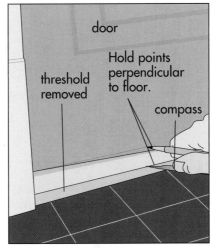

Scribe the bottom of a door.
If the bottom of a door is sticking, close it as far as possible. Set a compass to the correct height above the floor—usually the thickness of the threshold plus 1/8 inch for clearance. Hold the compass point on the floor and the pencil end of the compass on the door. Move the compass along the floor, scribing a parallel cutoff line on the door.

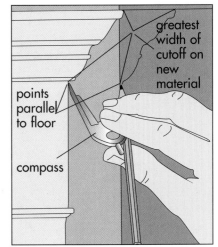

Mark for irregular cuts.
For a complicated contour cut, use a compass that can be tightened firmly so it won't collapse or expand as you trace the contour. Place the new material next to the object it will fit around. Set the compass to the greatest width to be cut off. Take care to hold the two compass points on the same plane (in this case, parallel to the floor) as you make the mark.

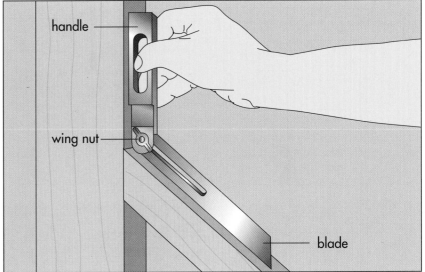

Use a T-bevel for odd angles.
If you want to duplicate an angle that is neither 45 nor 90 degrees, use a sliding T-bevel. Loosen the wing nut so the blade can be moved without difficulty. Hold the handle against one edge and move the blade until it rests firmly against the other edge. Tighten the wing nut firmly. The tool holds the angle you need, allowing you to transfer it to the wood you are cutting. When making an inside measurement, as shown *above*, extend the blade fully to ensure an accurate reading.

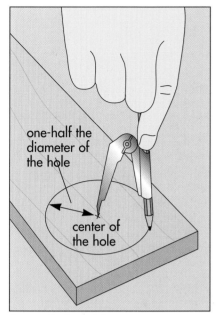

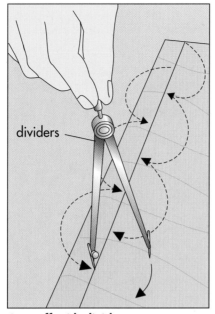

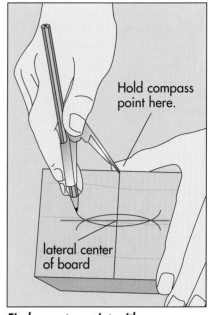

Draw circles with a compass.

To mark small circles—for boards that will be cut to accept pipes, lighting fixtures, etc.—a simple compass will do the job. Mark a spot at the center of the hole and set the compass width to one-half the diameter of the hole. For accuracy, be sure the compass is tightly clamped in position and hold it as perpendicular to the surface as possible.

Step off with dividers.

If you need to mark a series of equidistant points along a straight line, use dividers. Steel pins at the base of each leg grip the surface of the material you're measuring for good control. Use a swiveling motion as you step from one leg to the other leg.

Find a center point with a compass.

If you need to find the exact center point of a board, doing it with math can be confusing— what's half of $9\frac{3}{8}$ inches, for instance? To quickly find the center point, open your compass to a bit more than half the board's width and make two arcing marks as shown. The line between the points where the curved lines intersect is the center of the board.

Make a tool for larger circles.

A compass works well for small circles, but if you have to cut out for a sink or another large, round object, you will have to use a little ingenuity. Make your own compass out of a pencil, brad, and string. Be sure to hold the pencil vertical as you draw.

For greater accuracy, make a notch at one end of a small piece of wood. Nail the wood piece in place with a brad at the center of the circle. The notch holds the pencil in place for a smooth, accurate line.

Sometimes, you may be able to find a round household object, such as a can, a bucket, or a wastebasket, that is close enough to the correct size. Place it on the work and trace around it.

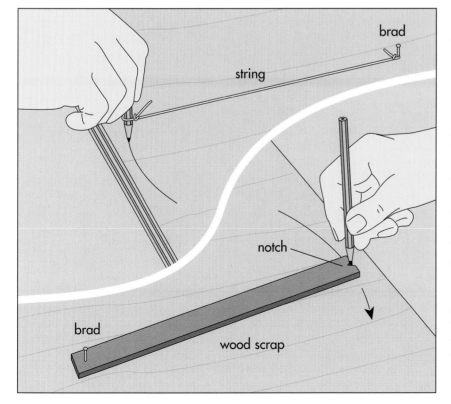

CUTTING WITH A CIRCULAR SAW

Chances are you will do most of your cutting with a circular saw. Whether cross-cutting 1-inch stock, ripping plywood, or cutting bricks with a masonry blade, you'll do the job better if you follow a few basic rules when using this versatile tool.

Whenever you cut, allow the saw to reach full operating speed, then slowly push the blade into the wood. Some carpenters look at the blade as they cut; others rely on the gunsight notch. Choose the method that suits you best. Avoid making slight turns as you cut. Instead, find the right path, and push the saw through the material smoothly. It will take some practice before you can do this consistently. This is a powerful tool with sharp teeth, so take care. It demands your respect.

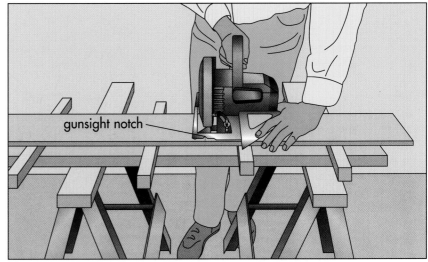

gunsight notch

Support the material properly.
Well-supported work results in clean, safe cuts. If the scrap piece is short, support the board on the nonscrap side. If the scrap is long, it could bind the blade or splinter as it falls away at the end of the cut. To achieve a neat cut and avoid saw kickback, support the lumber in four places. Even with such precautions, you may want to make two cuts: one to cut the work roughly to size, the other for the finish cut.

TOOLS TO USE

CHOOSING A CIRCULAR SAW AND BLADES

■ Choose a circular saw that is comfortable. It should have some heft, but should not be so heavy that it is difficult to maneuver. You should be able to see the blade and gunsight notch easily. Check for ease of depth and angle adjustments. (For more tips, see page 11.)

■ If you buy only one blade for a circular saw, choose a carbide-tipped combination blade that has at least 24 teeth. It works well for rough work and makes cuts clean enough for most finish work. For fine work, buy a plywood blade or a hollow-ground planer blade. For extensive remodeling jobs, get a second carbide-tipped blade that you can use when you may need to cut through nails or other rough materials.

CAUTION!
AVOIDING AND PREPARING FOR KICKBACK

It happens to even the most experienced carpenter: A blade binds, causing a circular saw to jump backward. Kickback can mar the lumber you are working on, and it is dangerous. Unsupported work often is the culprit. But also watch for these situations:

■ A dull blade will bind and cause the saw to kick. Change your blade if you have to push hard to make it cut.

■ Bending or twisting lumber will grab a blade. Sheets of plywood are particularly prone to this. Make sure it is evenly supported, like the 1× above.

■ Kickback also can occur when you back up while cutting or when you try to make a turn. If your cut is going off line, stop the saw, back up, and start again.

■ Occasionally, certain types of wood grain will grab the blade and cause a kickback. There's nothing you can do about this except be prepared.

■ Don't wear long sleeves and don't position your face near the circular saw.

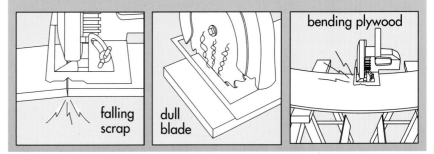

falling scrap

dull blade

bending plywood

EXPERTS' INSIGHT

SET THE BLADE DEPTH CORRECTLY

Before you make any cut, check to see that the blade is set to about ¼ inch deeper than the thickness of the wood. (Be sure to unplug the saw before you do this.) This may seem like a lot of bother, especially if you are constantly switching between 1× and 2× lumber, but here's why it is worth the trouble:

■ A saw blade that extends only slightly below the material will produce a much cleaner cut than a blade that extends way below the material.

■ The deeper the blade is set, the more prone it will be to binding and kickback, jeopardizing the work and your safety.

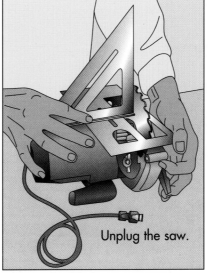

Unplug the saw.

Square the blade.

To square a blade, hold a speed square against the blade and adjust it. (Be sure to position the square between the teeth.) To test if your blade is square to the baseplate, crosscut a piece of 2× lumber. Flip the piece over and press cut edge against cut edge. If you see a gap at the top or the bottom, the blade is not square.

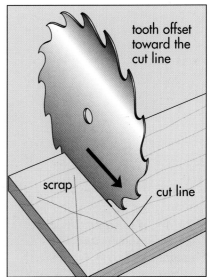

tooth offset toward the cut line

scrap

cut line

Align the blade with the cut line.

Once you have drawn an accurate cutoff line and have properly supported the board, position the saw blade to the scrap side of the line. The teeth on most circular saw blades are offset in an alternating pattern, half to the left and half to the right. When clamping a guide, align a tooth that points toward the cutoff line.

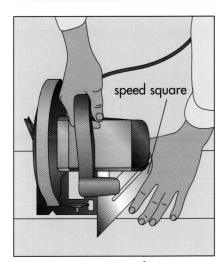

speed square

Use a square as a guide.

With practice, you will learn to cut accurately without using a guide. But for cuts that have to be precise, use a guide. For 90-degree cuts, a speed square works well because it's easy to hold stable. Align the blade, then slide the square into position against the saw's baseplate. Grab the board along with the square, so the square won't slip out of position.

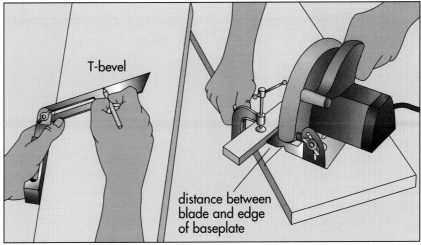

T-bevel

distance between blade and edge of baseplate

Use other guides for angle cuts.

With care, you can improvise a saw guide that will be as accurate as a miter box. Set a T-bevel to the desired angle (see page 34) and transfer the angle to the board.

Select a straight piece of 1× and clamp it along the cutting line as a saw guide. To offset the guide correctly, measure the distance between the blade and the edge of the saw's baseplate and clamp the

guide that distance from the cut line. It may take some experimenting before you get this correct. Be sure to align the blade to the correct side of the line.

You can use the same principle for long rip cuts. Clamp a straightedge—the factory edge of a 1× or a drywall square—onto the material, setting it back from the cut line to allow for the width of the saw's baseplate.

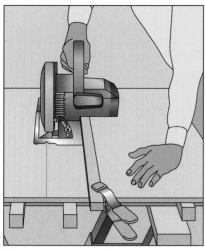

Support sheet goods.

Cut sheet goods with a carbide-tipped combination blade or a plywood-cutting blade for a smoother cut. It is important to support the sheet properly, or the blade will bind. You can do this by setting four 2× support pieces on the floor, a table, or a pair of sawhorses. Arrange two support pieces on either side of the cut line so that when the cut is complete, both pieces of the sheet are stable.

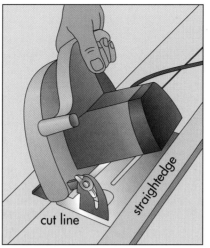

Use a guide.

Use a guide to make a straight, long cut. Get a straightedge that is as long as the material you are cutting—a straight 1×4 or the factory edge of a piece of plywood. Measure the distance from the edge of the saw's baseplate to the blade and clamp the guide that distance away from the cut line. Set the saw in place and check alignment with the cut line. Clamp the opposite end of the guide the same distance from the edge.

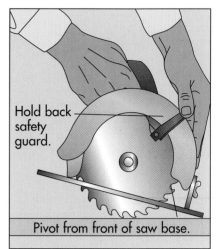

Make a plunge cut.

Use a plunge cut, also called a pocket cut, to make a hole or slit in the middle of a board or sheet. Set the blade to the correct depth. Retract the safety guard and tilt the saw forward, setting the front of the baseplate on your work. Start the saw and lower it slowly into the cut line until the base rests on the stock. Complete the cut.
Note: *Because you will be exposing the blade, any twist could result in a dangerous kickback. Be careful.*

USING A MITER BOX

A miter joint is made when two pieces of wood are angle-cut or bevel-cut at the same angle then joined to form a corner. Most often, two pieces that have been cut at 45 degrees are joined to make a 90-degree corner. Miter cuts must be precise. If they are off even one degree, the corner will be noticeably out of true.

The most inexpensive way to make angle or bevel cuts in narrow stock is to use a miter box—essentially a jig for holding the saw at the proper angle to the work. If you have a lot of joinery to cut, consider buying a power miter saw (see page 50).

Before placing the piece in the miter box, support it on a scrap of 1×4 or some other suitable material. This allows you to saw completely through the work

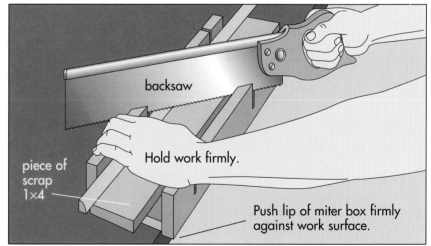

without marring the bottom of the miter box. Place the member against the far side of the miter box, positioned as it will be when in use, and make the cut with a backsaw. Hold the work firmly against the back of the box with your free hand.

If there's any trick to using a miter box, it's not in the cutting technique, but in correctly measuring and marking for the cut. Whenever possible, make your miter cut first, then cut the other end of the piece to the proper length with a straight cut.

CUTTING WITH A HANDSAW

Although you will probably do most of your cutting with power tools, there are times when a handsaw is more convenient. Learn the proper technique, and hand-cutting may turn out to be easier than you expected.

Make a crosscut with a handsaw.

To make a crosscut with a handsaw in narrow goods, set the blade's heel end (nearest the handle) at a 45-degree angle to the work. Set the teeth on the scrap side of the cut line. To make sure the blade doesn't wander, use your thumbnail as a guide. Pull the saw back toward you several times to start the cut. Don't force the blade; use the weight of the saw to start the cut while you guide it. Saw with a rocking motion, using a steeper angle at the beginning of the downstroke and a flatter angle at its completion. Again, don't force it; let the saw do the work.

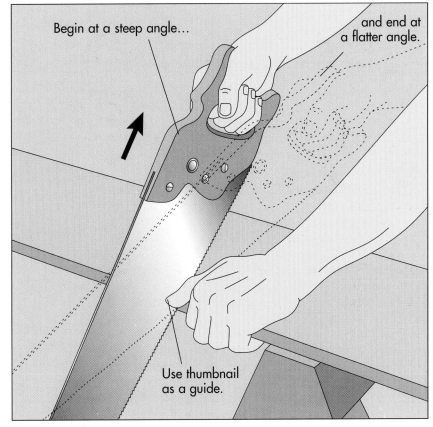

Begin at a steep angle...

and end at a flatter angle.

Use thumbnail as a guide.

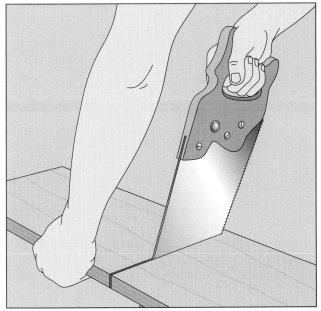

Finish the cut cleanly.

When you near the end of the cut, support the scrap end of the piece of wood. Grasp it firmly with your free hand, exerting a slight upward pressure to keep it from binding. This also will keep the piece from snapping and splintering on the last stroke.

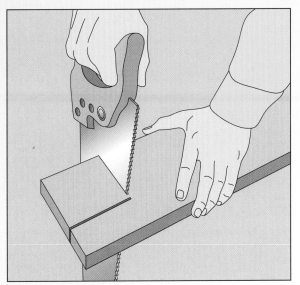

Make a cutout.

To notch the corner of a board, position the blade of the saw so it is perpendicular to the work as you near the end of each cut. In that way, the bottom of the board is cut the same distance as the top. Often it is helpful to reverse the position of the saw, as shown *above*.

MAKING INSIDE AND CONTOUR CUTS

Often you need to make a cut in the center of a piece of lumber or sheet goods or make a curved or irregularly shaped cut. These cuts require two basic steps. First you need to drill or plunge-cut an access hole in the material. Then you need to use a narrow-bladed tool that can handle curved cuts to follow the contours.

To begin an inside cut, you can use a circular saw to make a plunge cut (see page 38). You will need a sabersaw or handsaw to finish the job. If you find it difficult to make a precise plunge cut, use a drill and sabersaw—especially when the finished work will be highly visible.

Note: *Do not attempt to make a curved cut with a circular saw. Such a practice not only can damage your saw and saw blades, but it also can be dangerous.*

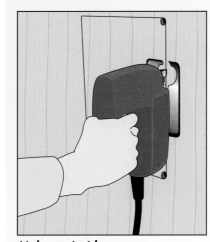
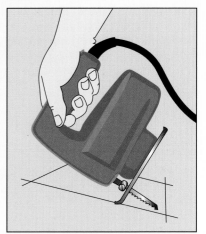

Make an inside cut.
How you start an inside cut depends on the material you're cutting. With lumber and sheet goods, the safest way is to drill a starter hole at each corner of the cutout, as close as possible to the cut lines. Insert the blade of a sabersaw or keyhole saw into one of the holes and complete the cut.

If you are experienced with a sabersaw, make a plunge cut. Tip the saw forward on its baseplate, as shown. Start the saw and slowly lower the blade into the wood along the cut line. A sabersaw blade tends to dance before cutting into the surface, which can badly mar your work. You may want to practice on a scrap of wood first.

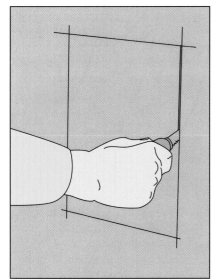
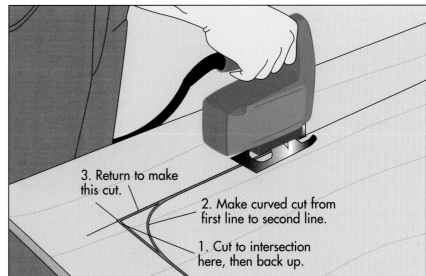

3. Return to make this cut.

2. Make curved cut from first line to second line.

1. Cut to intersection here, then back up.

Cut holes in drywall.
For a clean cut, score the paper face of the drywall with a knife before sawing it. Poke the tip of a drywall saw (a type of keyhole saw) into the drywall at a cut line. Either push or punch the saw handle with the heel of your hand.

Cut corners without a pilot hole.
You can maneuver a sabersaw around fairly tight corners, but don't try to make 90-degree turns. Use a three-step procedure to cut such corners. On your first approach to a corner, cut just up to the intersecting line. Carefully

back the saw up about 2 inches and cut a gentle curve over to the next cut line. Continue in this direction, supporting the scrap material as you cut, until the scrap piece is free. Then go back and finish trimming the corners with short, straight cuts.

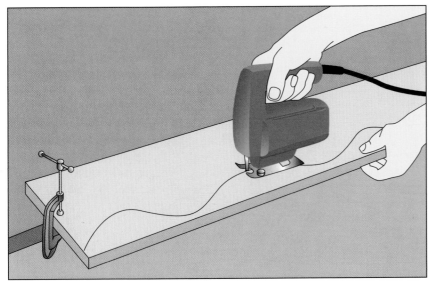

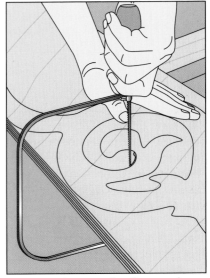

Cut curves with a sabersaw.

For most contour cuts, use a sabersaw. Once you get the knack of using this tool, you can cut curves that are as smooth as any line you can draw. Be sure the piece you are going to cut is stable; clamp it if necessary. Check that nothing is blocking the path of the blade underneath the piece you are cutting.

Turn the saw on, then begin the cut. Guide the saw slowly, without forcing the blade. One sharp turn can break a blade. If the saw begins to bog down or overheat, you're cutting too fast. If you wander from the line, don't try to make a correction with a sharp turn. Instead, back up and start again. Support the scrap material as you reach the end of each cut to prevent it from breaking off.

Use a coping saw for fine work.

For intricate cutting or scrollwork, use a coping saw. This hand tool allows you to set the blade in any direction in relation to its frame. To begin a cut from the inside of a board, remove the blade from the saw frame and reinstall it through a starter hole. For delicate cuts, install the blade with the teeth angled toward the handle so the saw cuts on the backstroke.

Use coping cuts for moldings.

When you're working with moldings, it's difficult to get perfectly matched mitered joints for inside corners, especially because the corners of walls often are not square. That's why professionals usually cope inside corner joints.

Start by cutting the first piece of molding at a 90-degree angle so it butts against the adjacent wall. To cope the overlapping piece, make an inside 45-degree miter cut, as shown. Use a coping saw to cut away the excess wood along the molding profile. Back-cut slightly (cut a little more off the back of the piece than the front) to ensure a neat fit. Whenever possible, make the cut on the coped end first, hold the piece in place, then mark for the cut on the other end.

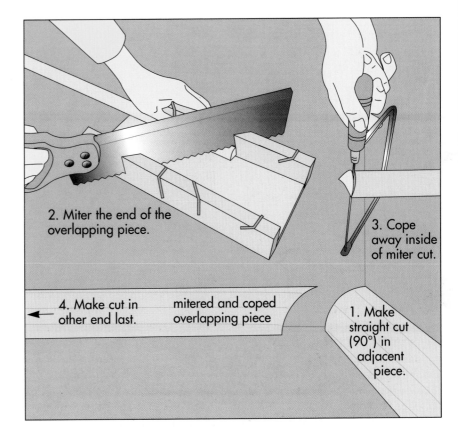

2. Miter the end of the overlapping piece.

3. Cope away inside of miter cut.

4. Make cut in other end last.

mitered and coped overlapping piece

1. Make straight cut (90°) in adjacent piece.

USING CHISELS

Although you may not use a chisel every day, it pays to keep a couple of them on hand. Nothing can replace a chisel for making mortises, dadoes, or notches. An old one often comes in handy for demolition jobs.

Whenever you pick up a chisel, keep both hands behind the cutting face of the blade. As you work, point the chisel away from your body. Because it takes two hands to operate a chisel, always clamp or anchor the material you're working on. Save yourself wasted effort and ruined materials by keeping your chisels sharp. A properly sharpened chisel should slice through paper easily.

TOOLS TO USE

SHARPENING NICKED OR BADLY WORN TOOLS

To sharpen a badly nicked or worn chisel, a single-cut file or a bench grinder works better than a whetstone.

■ To sharpen a chisel with a file, clamp the chisel tightly in a vise with the cutting edge pointing up. Remove nicks by filing nearly perpendicular to the chisel edge. Then hold the file at the same angle as the chisel bevel and file diagonally across the bevel. Work slowly and evenly to obtain a sharp edge. Remove burrs on the flat side with an oiled whetstone.

■ To remove nicks from a chisel's blade with a bench grinder, hold the chisel nearly perpendicular to the wheel and grind until the nicks disappear. Regrind the bevel, using the guide on the grinder to hold the chisel at the bevel angle. Go slowly: Never let the cutting edge blacken or get red hot.

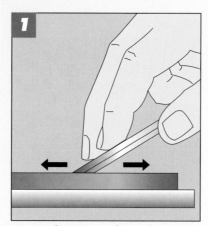

1. To sharpen with a whetstone, grind the cutting edge.
A dull chisel edge will look flat and reflect light. It also may have nicks in it. Drip a pool of oil on a whetstone. Brace the whetstone firmly on a flat surface. Hold the chisel bevel-face-down, at an angle slightly steeper than the bevel, so you are not grinding the entire beveled face. Grind by pressing gently and moving back and forth.

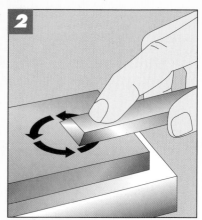

2. Smooth the flat side.
Turn the chisel over and lay its flat side on the whetstone. Add more oil if the stone is dry or if a thick paste has built up. Hone the flat side by pressing gently, moving the chisel with a circular motion. You don't want to grind a new cutting edge on this side; only remove the burrs created after grinding the beveled face.

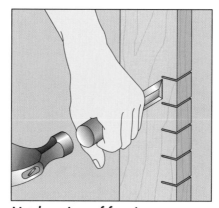

Notch a piece of framing.
Set your circular saw blade to the desired depth of the notch and make cuts at the top and bottom of the notch. If the notch is wide, make one or more cuts in the center of the notch as well. Position the chisel with the bevel outward. Begin cutting at a slight outward angle that gets flatter as you proceed.

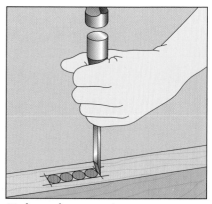

Make a deep mortise cut.
It is difficult to chisel deeply into a narrow board without splintering it. Begin by drilling a series of adjacent holes within the scored outline of the mortise. If possible, use a drill bit that is the same diameter as the width of the mortise. Finish the cut with a chisel, holding the beveled face toward the inside of the mortise as you gently tap.

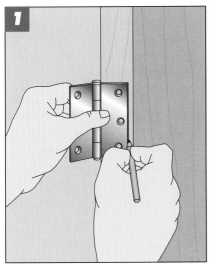

1. Mark to mortise for a hinge.

Do not attempt to mark a mortise for a hinge with a measuring device. Use the actual hinge as a template. Position it correctly on the edge of the door and mark its perimeter with a sharp pencil. (For an alternative method, see page 88.) Mark for the thickness of the mortise also.

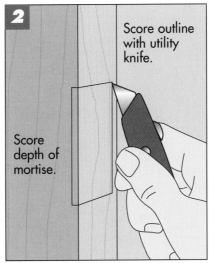

2. Score the lines.

To prevent the wood grain from splintering at the edges of chisel cuts, score the lines you have just marked by gently cutting with a sharp knife. Once the score lines have been established, go over them again with the knife until you have cut to the depth of the mortise. A butt marker also can be used to score lines (see page 88).

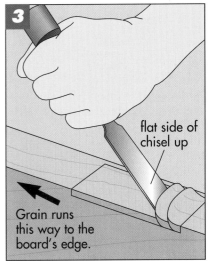

3. Chisel out the mortise.

Hold the chisel with the beveled face down at the angle shown. Whenever possible, cut in the direction in which the wood grain runs to the edge of the board. Otherwise, the chisel will follow the grain deeper down into the board than you intended. Drive the chisel to the depth of the mortise, making several slices across its width.

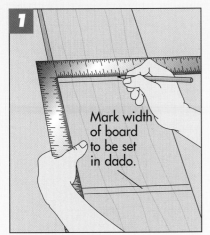

1. To make dado notches, first lay out the lines.

When laying out dado cuts across the width of a board, take extra care to draw lines that are straight and square and that mark the exact thickness of the boards that will be set into them. Use a framing or a smaller square to mark both the top and bottom of the cut.

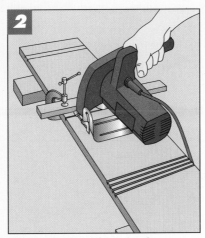

2. Cut lines with a circular saw.

Adjust your circular saw blade to the correct depth—usually one-third of the thickness of the board. Use a speed square (see page 37) or a clamp-on guide to ensure that you stay on the outline marks. After cutting the two outside lines for wide dadoes, make a series of passes through the center of each notch.

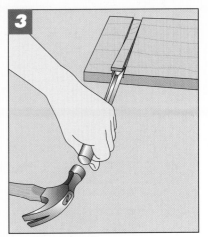

3. Chisel out the waste.

Using a chisel the same width or narrower than your dado notches, tap out the remaining slivers of wood. Start from one edge and work toward the middle, then work from the other side. Smooth the bottom of the notch by scraping it with your chisel, flat side down.

DRILLING

Some carpenters still haul out a brace and expandable auger bit when they can't find a spade bit of the right size. But now the electric drill usually is the tool of choice. Not only can you drill a hole of about any size with a variable-speed power drill, but you also can use a drill to drive screws into wood or metal, buff and grind, and even mix paint or mortar.

Some carpenters keep two drills on hand—one for drilling pilot holes, the other for driving screws. That way, they don't waste time changing bits. A power drill with a keyless chuck speeds up a bit change, although you may find bits slip during heavy-duty tasks.

For perfectly perpendicular holes, you'll need a drill press. But if you learn the techniques here and on the next three pages, you can bore holes that are straight enough for household carpentry.

EXPERTS' INSIGHT

CHOOSING A DRILL

■ Avoid buying a cheap drill with a ¼-inch chuck. It will not have the power you need and will soon burn out. One tipoff to a better-quality tool is the cord. Look for a long cord that flexes more like rubber than plastic.

■ A hammer drill, or a drill with a hammer option, bangs away at the material as it drills. It's useful when boring holes in concrete.

■ A cordless drill can make your work go more easily, but only if it is powerful enough to do most things that a corded drill can do.

■ Some drills are designed specifically for driving in drywall screws. These set the head of the screw at the required depth—deep enough to make an indentation, but not so deep that it damages the drywall.

■ Specialized tasks often require a high-speed drill (one with high revolutions per minute). For example, self-tapping steel stud screws (see page 97) require a drill rated to at least 2,500 rpm.

■ For heavy-duty work, choose a drill with a ½-inch chuck. This will run at fewer revolutions per minute, but will be more powerful than a standard ⅜-inch drill.

For additional information on choosing a drill, see page 11.

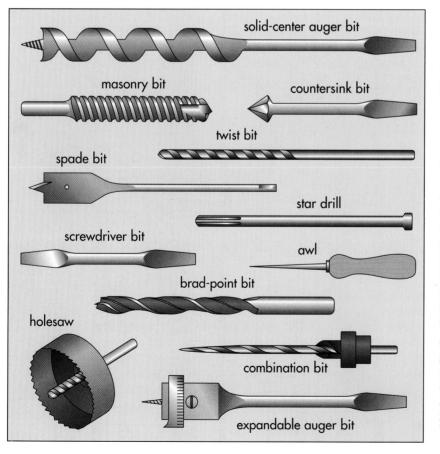

Choose the correct bit.
Shown at *left* are some of the more common drill bits. **Auger** bits, either solid-center or expandable, are designed to be used with a hand brace, as is a **screwdriver** bit. For holes ½ inch or smaller in diameter, use **twist** bits. A **brad-point** bit makes a cleaner hole than a twist bit. For holes from ½ to 1¼ inches in diameter, use a **spade** bit. For making holes in masonry or concrete, use a carbide-tipped **masonry** bit or a **star drill**, which you drive with a hammer. A **countersink** bit bores a shallow hole so you can set screw heads flush with or below the surface. A **combination** bit drills both a pilot hole and a countersink hole in one step. Use a simple **awl** to prepare the way for a small screw. For holes larger than 1¼ inches, and/or for drilling precise holes through tough materials, use a **holesaw**.

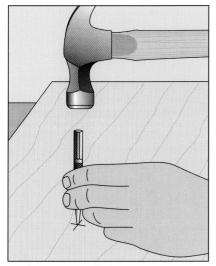

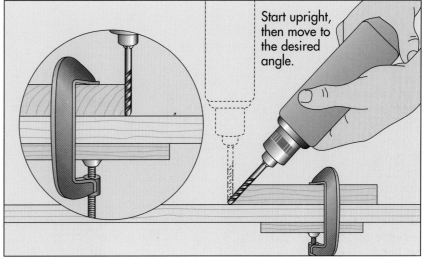

Make a starter hole.
Drill bits tend to skate away when you begin boring holes, so make a shallow starter hole with an awl or a center punch. In softwoods, a gentle tap on an awl with the palm of your hand will do the job. With hardwoods or metal, you may need to tap the center punch or awl with a hammer.

Improvise a guide.
Usually, you'll want to drill holes perpendicular to the board. Check the bit for square as it enters the material by clamping a piece of square-cut scrap lumber in place, as shown. With some drills, you can hold a square on the material and against the body of the drill.

Sometimes you'll want your bit to enter the material at an angle.

Fashion a guide by cutting the edge of a piece of scrap lumber to the desired angle of your hole. Clamp the guide so it aligns the tip of the bit exactly on your center mark. Begin the hole by drilling perpendicular to the surface. Once you have gone deep enough to keep the bit from skating away, shift the drill to the correct angle.

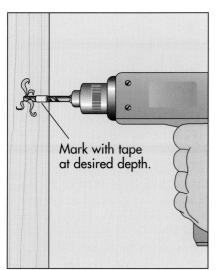

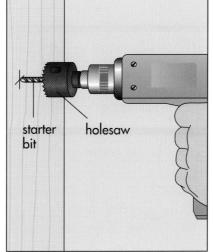

Mark the bit for depth.
When you want to drill one or more holes to a certain depth, wrap masking or electrical tape around your drill bit so the bottom edge of the tape contacts the surface of the material at the desired depth. Drill with gentle pressure. Back the bit out as soon as the tape touches the surface of the material.

Use a holesaw.
When drilling large-diameter holes with a holesaw, make a starter hole on your center mark to guide the starter bit. To ensure that the other side of the material doesn't splinter when the bit penetrates it, clamp a piece of scrap stock against the other side. Or, drill just far enough so the starter bit pokes through, then drill from the other side.

CAUTION!
AVOID DAMAGING YOUR DRILL BITS AND DRILL
Drilling is a simple procedure, but it's easy to dull or break a drill bit. Be careful not to overheat the bit; an overheated bit will become dull quickly. If you see smoke, stop drilling immediately. Pause once in a while and test the bit for heat by quickly tapping it with your finger.
If you own a homeowner-type drill rather than a professional model, it is not designed for constant use. If you feel the body of the drill heating up, stop and give it a rest, or you could burn it out.
Hold the drill firmly upright as you work. If you tip the tool while drilling, there's a good chance the bit will break.

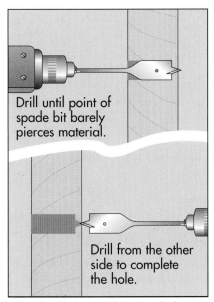

Drill until point of spade bit barely pierces material.

Drill from the other side to complete the hole.

Back up to pull wood particles out.

Clean particles from the flute.

Avoid splinters with a spade bit.
When using a spade bit, drill through the material until the tip of the bit begins to poke out the back side of the material. Carefully reverse the bit out of the hole. Complete the hole by drilling from the other side, using the pilot hole you've just made.

Keep particles from clogging hole.
When you drill deep holes into thick material, wood particles build up in the hole, clogging the bit and causing it to bind. Don't force the bit in farther than it wants to go or you will burn it out. Instead, feed the bit into the wood slowly and back out of the hole frequently with the drill

motor still running. This will pull trapped wood particles to the surface. If you're working with sappy or wet wood, shavings may clog the flute of the bit. If this happens, stop the drill, and use the tip of a nail to scrape out the shavings. If the bit jams, reverse the drill rotation. Pull the bit straight up and out.

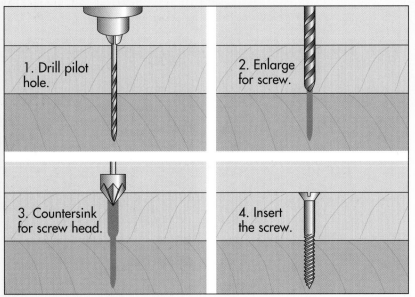

1. Drill pilot hole.

2. Enlarge for screw.

3. Countersink for screw head.

4. Insert the screw.

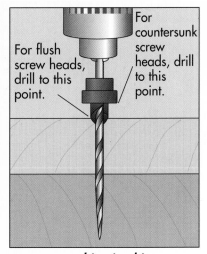

For flush screw heads, drill to this point.

For countersunk screw heads, drill to this point.

For the best fit, drill three holes...
When you use wood screws to fasten two pieces of material together, take the time to provide clearance for the screw to ensure easy driving and to avoid splits. Using a bit that is slightly smaller than the screw, drill through the top and bottom piece. Then select

a bit that is as thick as the screw shank and drill through the top board. The screw should slide easily through this top hole and grip tightly as it passes into the smaller hole. Use a countersink bit to bore a space for the screw head. When you drive the screw, it will fit without cracking the wood.

or use a combination bit.
If you're driving a lot of screws, buy a combination countersink-counterbore bit, which drills three holes in one action. Be sure to get the correct bits for the screws you will be driving. If you want the screw head to be flush with the surface, drill until the spot marked on the bit is even with the surface. To counterbore the screw head, drill deeper.

EXPERTS' INSIGHT

DRILLING THROUGH METAL

If you need to make a hole in metal, it is best to use a high-quality titanium bit. But if you work carefully, you can drill through metal with any sharp twist bit. The trick is to keep the bit and the metal lubricated with light oil at all times. If the bit is dry for even a couple of seconds while drilling, it can burn out and become dull.

Before you start, drip motor oil onto the bit and the spot to be drilled. Add oil as you work. Take your time, stopping often to make sure the bit is oiled and not overheating.

If you need to drill a hole larger than ¼ inch in diameter, drill a smaller hole first, then use a bigger bit.

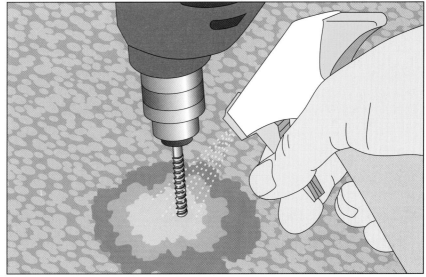

Drill into masonry and concrete.
Use a masonry bit when drilling into brick or concrete surfaces. Usually, brick is easy to drill into and concrete is more difficult. Check the bit often to make sure it's not overheating. If you see smoke, stop immediately.

Here is a trick that works surprisingly well: Spray the bit and the hole with window cleaner as you work. Not only does this keep the bit cool, but the foaming action of the cleaner brings debris up and out of the hole.

Occasionally when drilling into concrete, you will run into an especially hard spot (usually a rock embedded in the concrete). Take the bit out, insert a masonry nail or thin cold chisel, and bang with a hammer to crack the rock and give your bit a place to grab. If you have a lot of masonry drilling to do, buy a hammer drill, which bangs away as you drill.

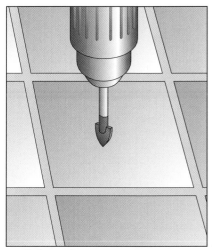

Drill through ceramic tile.
Wall tiles are usually soft, but floor tiles can be very tough. Nick the surface of the tile just enough so the bit will not wander as you drill. Keep the bit and the hole lubricated with a few drops of oil. Use a masonry bit or a special tile bit like the one shown *above*.

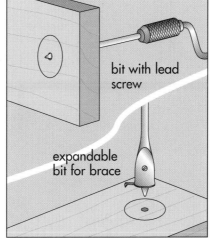

bit with lead screw

expandable bit for brace

Use a brace and expandable bit.
A brace is an old-fashioned tool that works faster than you may expect. To drill large diameter holes, bore until the lead screw of the bit pokes through the material. Then drill through from the other side. To get more pressure on the brace, hold its head against your body and lean into the work.

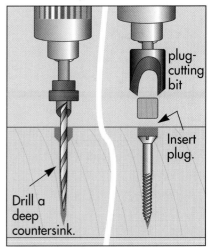

plug-cutting bit

Insert plug.

Drill a deep countersink.

Bore and plug for a finished look.
For a handcrafted appearance, drill pilot holes then drill a wooden plug using a plug-cutting bit. Drive the screw in, squirt a little white glue into the hole, and tap in the plug. Allow the plug to stick out slightly. After the glue has dried, chisel and sand the plug flush with the surface.

USING A TABLESAW

When shopping for a tablesaw, use a straightedge to check the table; it should be a perfectly flat plane. If the table has extensions, make sure they are flat as well. A small, lightweight tablesaw is handy if you need to move it around often. However, the smaller table area makes it more difficult to use, and you will have a hard time making accurate cuts on large pieces of material.

The fence of a tablesaw should move smoothly along its guide rails and lock firmly and exactly parallel to the blade.

If possible, turn the saw on and watch the blade. There should be no hint of a wobble. A belt-driven tablesaw works more smoothly and lasts longer than one with direct drive.

EXPERTS' INSIGHT

TABLESAW, RADIAL-ARM SAW, OR POWER MITER SAW?

■ A tablesaw and a power miter saw make an ideal combination. With a tablesaw, you can make straight, long cuts with ease. A tablesaw also is superior for cutting dadoes. With a power miter saw, you can crosscut long narrow pieces easily—a task that can be tricky with a tablesaw.

■ A radial-arm saw does the jobs of a tablesaw and power miter saw, but not quite as well. It crosscuts with less precision than the miter saw. Cutting angles other than 90 degrees may be a problem. Making long rip cuts in sheets of plywood also is difficult.

CAUTION!
SAFETY MEASURES FOR A TABLESAW

Because a tablesaw runs so smoothly and seems so stable, it's easy to lose safety-consciousness while working with one. A tablesaw is a tool worthy of respect. Many professionals have had parts of fingers cut off by a tablesaw blade.
Always keep your fingers well away from the blade. Never wear long sleeves or loose clothing. Never reach across the saw blade while it is running. Keep push sticks and an anti-kickback featherboard handy and develop the habit of using them (see page 49). Turn the saw off when you need to free a piece of wood that has become stuck.

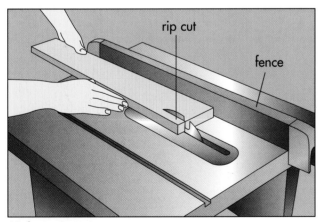

Make a rip cut.
Check that the fence is perfectly parallel to the blade by measuring the space between the blade and the fence at the front and the rear of the blade. Set the blade depth so it is ¼ inch above the top of the board. Start the motor and allow it to reach full speed. Hold the lumber against the fence so the wood glides smoothly and is flush against it at all points as you push it forward. Never allow your fingers to come within 6 inches of the blade; use a push stick when you come to the end of the cut (see page 49).

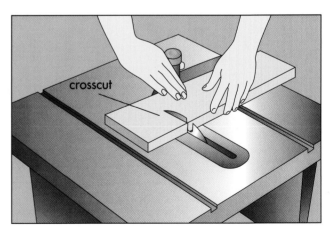

Make a crosscut.
Make sure the miter gauge is exactly perpendicular to the blade; slip it into its channel and square it using the edge of the table as a guide. Set the blade depth ¼ inch above the board and start the motor. Hold the board firmly against the miter guide and slide it toward the blade. Hold the board only at the miter gauge. If you hold the wood on both sides of the cut, the blade may bind, causing a dangerous kickback. Keep your fingers well away from the blade.

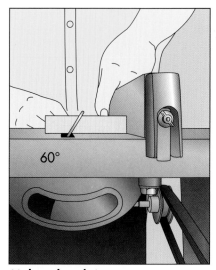

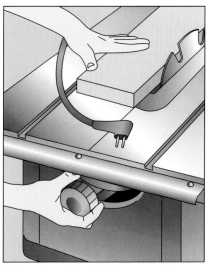

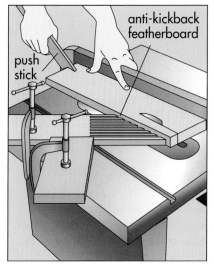

Make a bevel rip cut.

To set the bevel, use the saw gauge or mark the bevel angle on the butt end of the board and tilt the blade until it aligns with the mark. Hold the board against the blade at the correct location, slide the fence against the board, and lock the fence in position. Follow the same procedures as for a rip cut (see page 48).

Always set the height correctly.

Before every cut, adjust the blade depth so it is about $\frac{1}{4}$ inch above the top of the board you are cutting. This makes a cleaner cut and helps avoid binding and a dangerous kickback. If you are cutting a sheet of plywood that is warped, you may need to raise the blade higher, so it cuts through the sheet completely at all points. Always unplug the tablesaw before making blade adjustments.

Use push sticks and featherboard.

To make an anti-kickback featherboard, cut one end of a 16-inch-long 1×6 at 60 degrees, then cut 8-inch-long slots $\frac{1}{4}$ inch apart on the angled end. When clamped as shown *above,* it ensures a straight cut and prevents kickback in case the blade binds. Make push sticks out of 1× lumber or $\frac{1}{2}$-inch plywood and use them whenever you need to hold the board within 6 inches of the blade.

Cut dadoes, rabbets, and tenons.

With a dado blade, you can make a variety of groove sizes. With a regular dado blade, sandwich a combination of chippers between the two outside cutter blades to get your desired width. To set the blade to the desired depth, mark the depth on the board and hold it next to the blade as you adjust it. Adjustable dado blades dial to the desired width.

If you need to make a groove wider than the dado blade, make repeated passes, moving the board a little less than the width of the blade for each pass.

On a tablesaw, you will not be able to see the cut as you make it, so test your settings on a scrap piece to make sure the dado is the correct width and depth. Then make the real cut.

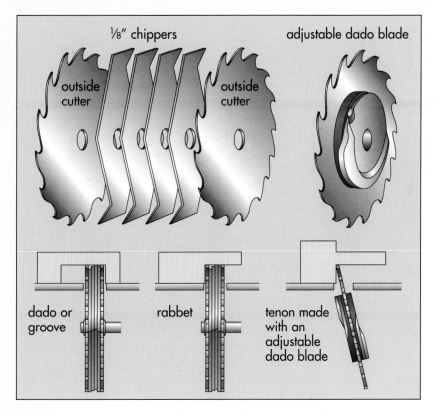

USING A RADIAL-ARM OR POWER MITER SAW

A radial-arm saw works best for crosscutting wood, but you can use it for ripping as well as long as you take it slowly and use precautions (see below right). With attachments available on some models, you can use a radial-arm saw as a router or a sander.

A radial-arm saw table is made of particleboard or plywood rather than metal because the saw blade must cut into the table slightly to cut boards completely. When the tabletop becomes shredded after years of use, you should replace it. The fence, usually a piece of 1×2, needs to be replaced more often.

A power miter saw is designed for two purposes only: miter-cutting and crosscutting small-width boards (usually 1×6 or smaller). Highly portable, a power miter saw sets up easily on a couple of sawhorses. It's ideal for cutting molding on the spot.

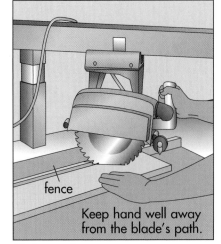

fence

Keep hand well away from the blade's path.

Make a miter cut or crosscut.
Test your saw for accuracy by cutting scraps at 45 and 90 degrees and adjust the fence or the saw if necessary. To make the cut, hold the board firmly against the fence. Make sure the board is fully supported and lies flat on the table. Pull the saw toward you, cutting the board so the saw kerf is on the scrap side of the line.

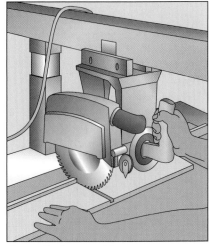

Cut a dado or rabbet.
To cut a notch for a dado or rabbet, raise the blade to the desired height; test the cut depth on a scrap. Check that the board lies flat; any warp will distort the cut. Cut on each side of the notch, then make a series of cuts in the interior. Clean out the notch with a chisel. If you have a lot of notching to do, use dado blades.

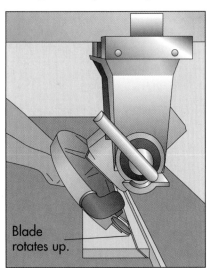

Blade rotates up.

Make a rip cut or beveled rip cut.
Turn the saw so the blade rotates up against the board, the opposite of a crosscut or dado cut. Start the saw with the blade slightly raised above the tabletop, then lower it to the cut line. To avoid kickback, hold the board firmly as you feed it into the blade. Pull the board through the blade to finish the cut.

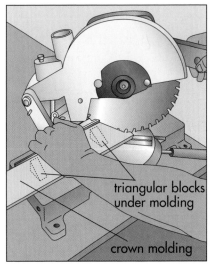

triangular blocks under molding

crown molding

Cut molding with a chopsaw.
Hold the piece firmly against the fence, start the saw, and lower the blade to make the cut. In many cases, the cut will not begin at the edge of a board, but in the middle; make your marks accordingly. When cutting crown molding, hold wood at the correct angle with triangular blocks.

CAUTION!
DEVELOP SAFETY HABITS
Radial-arm or power miter saws can be extremely dangerous. Not only can you cut yourself with the blades, but a radial-arm saw almost certainly will kick a board back at bullet-like speed if you are not careful. Develop these safety habits:
■ *Never remove the saw guard. Take the time to adjust the guard for maximum safety before making each cut.*
■ *When ripping boards with a radial-arm saw, use a push stick and featherboard like those for a tablesaw (see page 49). Also, stand to the side of the board, so if it does shoot back, it won't hit you.*
■ *Keep work well supported so the blade will not bind.*

USING A ROUTER

With the versatility and power of a router, you can custom-design and mill lumber to your own specifications. In addition to choosing among a wide variety of bits (shown *below*), you can set your bit to the depth of cut that suits you. Often, it's possible to save money by milling your own lumber rather than buying expensive moldings. For rounding off edges, a router produces a far more professional-looking finish than does a rasp or sander.

CAUTION!
BITS ARE SHARP!
Most of the time, you will not even see your router bit as you work. Don't let that lull you into complacency: A router's sharp bit, rotating at tremendous speeds, can do a lot of damage in a millisecond. Keep your hands well away from the work.

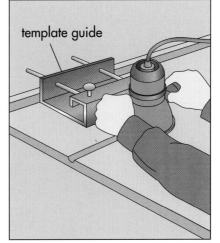

Use a guide.
You can make accurate cuts using a router guide. Sometimes a simple straightedge will suffice; just hold the baseplate tight against it as you cut. A template guide like the one shown allows you to follow a precut template. You may want to purchase a router table, which holds the router in an upside-down position; you can adjust and operate it much as you would a tablesaw.

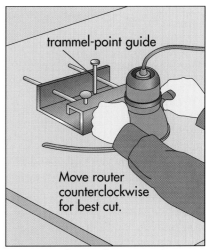

Move router counterclockwise for best cut.

Use specialty guides.
A variety of guides is available for special purposes. To cut smooth circles or curves, use a trammel-point guide like the one shown. A router bit spins clockwise, so you will get the best results if you move the router counterclockwise. You also can buy guides for cutting dovetail joints or hinge mortises.

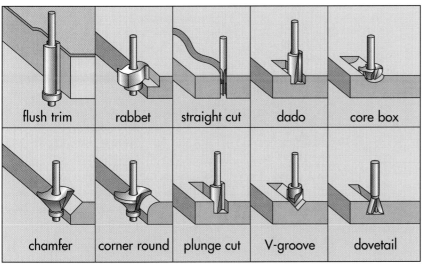

Choose among many bits.
Piloted bits, such as the **flush trim, rabbet, chamfer,** and **corner round**, are self-guiding; you don't need to use a guide or template when cutting with them. Use these bits to shape edges of boards or to final-cut laminates after they have been applied. Bits with ball-bearing guides usually work more smoothly.

The other bits shown require a guide or a steady hand. You can use two or more bits in succession to make intricate shapes.

EXPERTS' INSIGHT

CHOOSING A ROUTER
■ As a general rule, the more power a router has, the cleaner and faster it will cut. Get one that is at least 1 horsepower. A variable-speed router has some advantages because some bits are designed to be used at lower speeds than others.
■ Buy a model that can be attached to a table easily or that has a variety of guides you can assemble quickly. You don't want to spend half your work time setting up the router.
■ Be sure you can change bits quickly and adjust the router depth easily.

NAILING

The quickest way to make a job look shoddy and amateurish is to make a nailing mistake that mars the wood. All your careful measuring and cutting will be for naught if the wood ends up with "smiles" and "frowns" made by a hammer that missed the nail, or if you bend a nail while driving it.

Professional carpenters make nailing look easy—and for good reason. When properly done, pounding a nail home is not a struggle, but is done with smooth, fluid motions. You may never be as fast at nailing as professionals because they get plenty of practice, but you can learn to drive in nails accurately without damaging the material or yourself.

EXPERTS' INSIGHT

GETTING THE HOLDING POWER YOU NEED

■ How well a nail will hold in wood depends on how much of its surface contacts the wood. The longer and thicker the nail, the better it will hold.

■ When possible, use the Rule of Three: A nail should be three times as long as the thickness of the board being fastened. Two-thirds of the nail then will be in the second board to which you are fastening the first one. If the nail must penetrate through dead space or drywall, increase the nail length by that distance.

■ A thick nail holds better, but not if it splits the wood. In that case, most of its holding power is lost. Special nails, such as ring-shank and cement-coated nails, hold better than standard nails. A headed nail holds better than a finish nail.

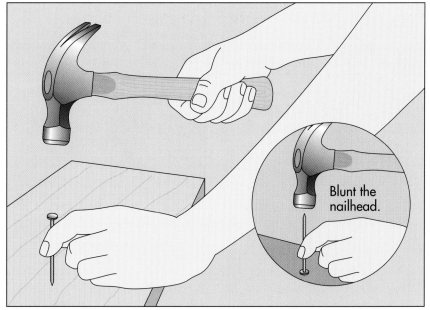

Blunt the nailhead.

Set the nail.
Practice on scrap pieces before you pound nails into finished work. To ensure that the hammer strikes the nail and not your fingers and that the nail will be driven into the board squarely, grasp the nail near its head and the hammer near the end of the handle. Lightly tap the nail until it stands by itself.

If you must drive a nail near the end of a board, drill a pilot hole or turn the nail upside down and blunt its point with a hammer. Either technique will reduce the risk of splitting the wood.

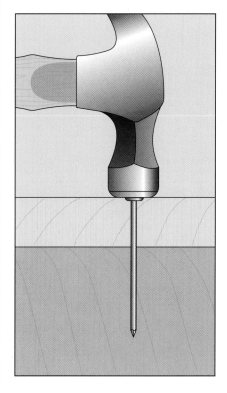

Use proper nailing techniques.
Once the nail is set in place, remove your hand from it. Keep your eye on the nail as you swing the hammer, letting the weight of the hammer head do the driving.

Beginners tend to hold a hammer stiffly and keep their shoulders stiff, swinging from the elbow. This leads to a tired, sore arm and to mistakes. Loosen up. Your whole arm should move as you swing from the shoulder. Keep your wrist loose so the hammer can give a final "snap" at the end of each blow. The entire motion should be relaxed and smooth.

With the last hammer blow, push the head of the nail flush or nearly flush with the surface of the wood. The convex shape of the hammer face allows you to do this without marring the surface.

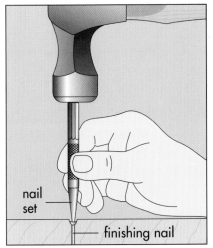

Countersink finishing nails.

In most cases, it's best to drive the heads of finishing or casing nails below the surface. You can fill the hole with wood putty later. This actually doesn't take all that long and leads to a much better-looking finish than nails driven flush. Hold a nail set against the nailhead and tap it in.

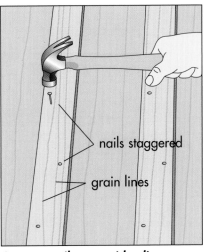

Stagger nails to avoid splits.

When driving several nails along the length of a board, stagger them so you don't split the board. The idea is to avoid pounding neighboring nails through the same grain line; two nails will stress the grain twice as much as one nail. If the work will be visible, stagger the nails in a regular pattern.

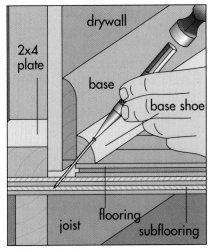

Drill pilot holes.

When you nail within 2 inches of the end of a board or into hardwood, drill pilot holes to avoid splitting the wood. Pilot holes should be slightly smaller than the diameter of the nail. When attaching a base shoe, drive nails into pilot holes so they miss the flooring, which needs room to expand and contract with changes in temperature and humidity.

EXPERTS' INSIGHT

USING MASONRY NAILS

■ Masonry nails offer a quick way to attach materials to concrete, brick, and masonry block. With flat-style masonry nails, be sure to turn the nail in the direction of the grain so it's less likely to split the wood.

■ You can use a standard hammer, but the job is easier with a heavy mallet. Hold the board in place, and drive the masonry nail through it. Once the nail hits the masonry surface, strike it with hard strokes. With subsequent nails, check to see if you have dislodged any nails; you may have to put in more.

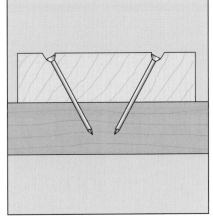

Skew nails for a stronger hold.

In situations where you cannot use as long a nail as you would like, drive nails in at an angle. Drive in one nail at about a 60-degree angle in one direction, then drive in another one in the opposite direction. The skewed nails will work together, making it difficult for the board to pull loose. Set the nailheads into the surface for a finished appearance.

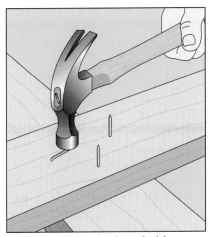

Clinch nails for the best hold.

If looks are not important, but strength is, use nails about 1 inch longer than the thickness of the pieces you're fastening. Drive in the nails, then turn the boards over and bend the exposed portion of the nails so they are nearly flush with the surface and parallel to the wood grain. The resulting joint will be extremely difficult to pull apart.

FASTENING WITH SCREWS

It's not hard to see why screws fasten so well. The threads grip wood fibers in a way that a smooth nail cannot. When the screw is driven home, the threads exert tremendous pressure against the screw head to hold the fastener firmly in place. With the right tools (see box below), driving screws can be almost as quick as nailing. If you make a mistake, it's easy to remove a screw without damaging your work. Screws must be driven with care, however. If you do not start out straight, there is no way to correct the mistake as you continue driving the screw. Without a pilot hole, the screw may split the wood and the screw will not hold securely. If the pilot hole is too large, again, the screw will not grip well.

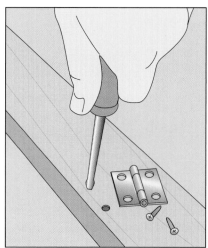

Make a starter hole with an awl.
Small screws seldom require pilot holes (see the box, below right). However, they do need a starter hole. Poke a hole with a scratch awl. Give it a few twists, back it out, and you're ready to drive in the screw.

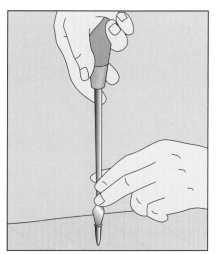

Drive with a hand screwdriver.
Start screws by holding the screwdriver handle with one hand and the screwdriver blade with the other. Don't hold the screw. If the screw is spinning around and not going into the wood, put two hands on the handle to apply more pressure.

TOOLS TO USE

Power-driven screws hold tightly, go in quickly, and are removed easily. Here are some tools that make working with them even more convenient.
■ A variable-speed, reversible drill starts the screws slowly and removes them if necessary.
■ With a magnetic sleeve, screws stick to the bit, making it easy to drive them in hard-to-reach places. Changing bit tips is easy; simply press them into the sleeve.
■ Have on hand a collection of drill bit tips, particularly #1 and #2 Phillips bits and some slotted bits as well.
■ Consider buying square-headed screws and bits. These bits fit into and grab the screw slot better than Phillips-head and slotted screws.

slotted screw bit

Power-drive slotted screws.
Even a few screws can take a long time to drive by hand, so consider using a drill with a screwdriver bit. When driving slotted screws, take care that the bit does not wander partway out of the slot, or you could damage the surface into which you are screwing. Don't drive screws too quickly, or the bit may slip out of the slot. Maintain firm, even pressure as you work.

EXPERTS' INSIGHT

WHEN DO YOU NEED A PILOT HOLE?

If there is a danger of cracking the wood, you should always drill a pilot hole, no matter how small the screw. For instance, if the wood is brittle or if you will be driving a screw near the end of a board, almost any screw can split the wood. But if you are drilling into a sound board at a spot 2 inches or more from its end, it usually will be safe to drive in a No. 6 or thinner screw without a pilot hole. If you are drilling into plywood or framing lumber, you should be able to drive No. 8 screws without pilot holes. For advice on selecting the correct-size bit, see page 25.

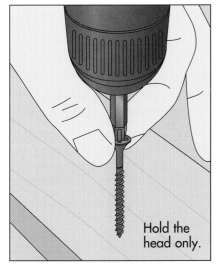

Use Phillips-head drywall screws.

You can buy drywall screws by the pound at bargain prices and drive them into most materials in which you would use nails. If you use a magnetic sleeve, place the screw on the bit first, then set the tip of the screw in place on the material. If you need to hold the screw to keep it from wandering, hold the head only, not the sharp threads.

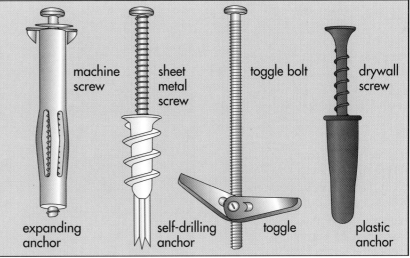

Attach items to walls with special wall fasteners.

If you need to attach something to a wall, the ideal way is to drive a screw into a stud. But often that's not possible. The screws and bolts shown *above* are designed to hold items firmly in drywall or plaster walls. To use **expanding anchors** and **plastic anchors**, drill holes and tap the unit into the wall; the

anchor will spread and grip as you tighten the screw. Use **self-drilling anchors** only in drywall. You don't need to drill a hole; just screw them in and insert a screw. To use a **toggle bolt**, drill a hole large enough for the folded-back toggles to fit through. Push the toggles through the hole, and turn the bolt until the toggles snug up to the back side of the wall.

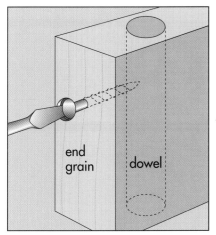

Screw into end grain.

When a fastener is driven into the end grain of a board, it will not hold as well as it does across the grain because it runs parallel to the grain rather than at an angle to it. Use a longer screw than you usually would. Where holding power is critical, drill a hole and install a dowel, as shown, into which you can drive the screw.

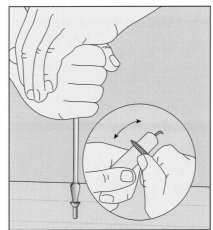

Deal with hard-to-drive screws.

If the going gets tough, the screw may stop turning. Exert pressure on the screwdriver with the palm of one hand and turn it with the other. If you still can't drive it, remove the screw and drill a slightly larger pilot hole. Another solution is to lubricate the threads with candle wax and try again.

EXPERTS' INSIGHT

FASTENING TO METAL WITH SCREWS

■ For fastening thin sheet metal or soft metal, such as brass, you can use one of several types of self-tapping sheet-metal screws (see page 97). Simply drive the screw in; it makes its own path with a metal-cutting point.

■ For heavier metals, drill a pilot hole using the techniques for drilling through metal (see page 47). Then install a sheet-metal screw.

■ For metal ⅛ inch or thicker and where you want an extra-strong joint, buy a drill-and-tap kit. With this, you can make a machine-threaded hole that will accept a machine bolt.

FASTENING WITH BOLTS

Nails and screws depend on friction between the fastener and the wood to do their job. When you tighten a nut on a bolt, however, you're actually clamping adjoining members together, producing the sturdiest of all joints. All types of bolts require a hole bored through both pieces being joined together. Here's information about installing machine and carriage bolts. For help with toggle bolts and other anchors, see page 55.

> **CAUTION!**
> Overtightening bolts can strip threads and damage wood, reducing the holding power of the bolt. Tighten the nut and bolt firmly against the wood, give them another half turn, then stop.

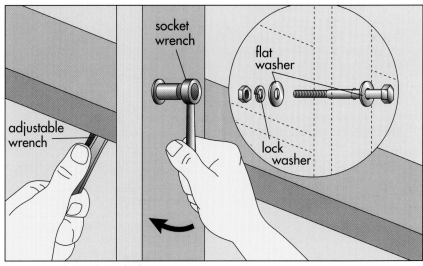

Fasten with machine bolts.

Machine bolts have hexagonal heads and threads running partway or all the way along the shank. When fastening two pieces of wood together, slip a flat washer onto the bolt and slide the bolt through the holes in both pieces of material. Add another flat washer, then a lock washer. Screw the nut on and tighten it. The flat washer keeps the nut and the bolt head from biting into the wood. The lock washer prevents the nut from coming loose. Use two wrenches to draw the nut down onto the bolt: one to steady the nut, the other to turn the bolt head.

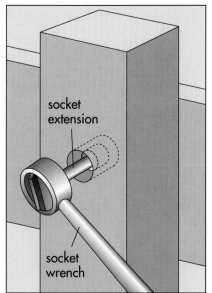

Tighten a countersunk bolt head.

To install a machine bolt in a hard-to-get-at place or when you have to countersink the bolt head, use a socket wrench with a socket extension to reach into the recess. Hold the nut with another wrench.

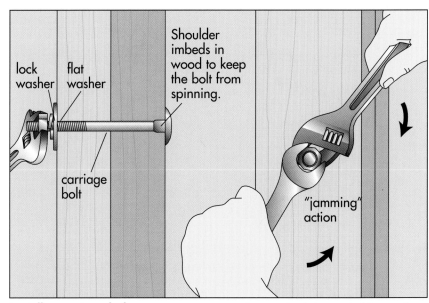

Install a carriage bolt.

A carriage bolt has a plain, round head. Insert it into the hole and tap the head flush with the surface. Slip a flat washer, a lock washer, and a nut onto the bolt. Tighten the nut. The square or hexagonal shoulder under the bolt head keeps the bolt from spinning as the nut is tightened. No washer is needed under the head.

The lock washer should keep the bolt from working loose. As added protection, you can thread another nut onto the bolt, snug it against the first, then "jam" the two together by turning them in opposite directions.

REMOVING NAILS AND SCREWS

Mistakes are a part of every carpenter's day. In fact, knowing how to undo mistakes is one of the hallmarks of an experienced carpenter, and that necessitates a good knowledge of how to remove nails and screws. Whether you're correcting mistakes, disassembling an old structure, or recycling used lumber, you'll find it's worth it to learn how to remove old fasteners quickly and neatly.

Removing screws often is just a matter of reversing your drill and screwing the old fastener out. However, you may be faced with a stripped head or an extra-tight screw (see page 58).

Most commonly, you'll be faced with removing nails. Don't just start whacking away in frustration, or you'll damage the wood. Use these methods and accept that nail removal is a normal part of a carpenter's job.

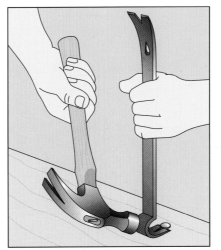

Pry with a flat bar.
If the head of the nail has not been set into the wood, it may be possible to shoehorn a flat bar under it and pry the nail up. Tap the notch of the chisel-like head of the bar under the nailhead and pull back on the bar. Because of its smooth, flat body, a pry bar makes only a slight indentation in the board as you remove the nail.

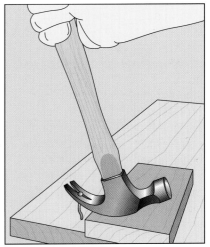

Use a wood block.
There are two good reasons for using a wood block when removing a nail. First, the raised height gives your hammer extra leverage, making it much easier to pull the nail out. Second, the block protects your work. Without it, the head of the hammer would dig in and make an unsightly indentation.

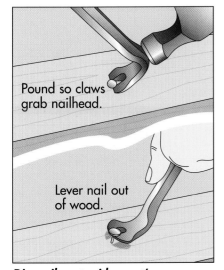

Pound so claws grab nailhead.

Lever nail out of wood.

Dig nails out with a cat's paw.
A cat's paw removes nails that are embedded deeply in lumber. Its drawback is that it also must bite deeply into the wood to grip the nailhead. Place the clawed tip behind the nailhead at a 45-degree angle. Pound the claws under the nailhead, pry the nail partway out, then use a hammer and block.

Tap out to release nails.

Tap in to expose nailheads.

Pound out board to loosen nails.
If you have access to the back side of the joined material, strike the joint from behind, then hammer the members back together from the front. This usually pops the nailheads out far enough for you to get hold of them with your hammer claw.

tight-work hacksaw

Cut the nails.
Where access is tight, sometimes you can disjoin two members by sawing through the nails. If you have a reciprocating saw with a metal-cutting blade, this will be easy. Otherwise, use a tight-work hacksaw. After you break the joint, use a nail set to force the heads out, then remove the nails.

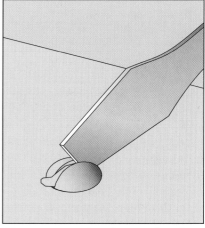

Punch through and pry.

To avoid splitting molding, punch the finishing nails that hold it in place through the molding with a nail set. Try not to make the hole larger; use a small-diameter nail set. Pound the head of the finishing nail deeply into the molding. You'll feel the board come loose. Once the nails are punched through, pry off the molding with a putty knife or chisel, taking care not to mar the wood.

Clean out a painted screw head.

When removing old screws that have been painted, take the time to clean the paint out of the slots. If you don't clean the head, you may strip the screw head, making it even more difficult to remove. Place a screwdriver as shown *above,* and tap with a hammer.

EXPERTS' INSIGHT

REMOVING OLD SCREWS

Here are some tips for removing stubborn old screws:

■ For a slotted screw that has been stripped so much that a screwdriver can't get a good hold, deepen the slot by cutting into it with a hacksaw.

■ Extremely tight screws often can be loosened with heat. Hold the tip of a soldering gun against the screw head for a minute or two, then try it.

■ For stripped Phillips-head screws, it sometimes helps to drill a small hole in the center of the head to give the screwdriver more to grab onto.

■ For an extremely stubborn screw, buy a screw and bolt extracting tool. Drill a small hole in the screw head, insert the tool, turn it with a wrench, and twist the screw out.

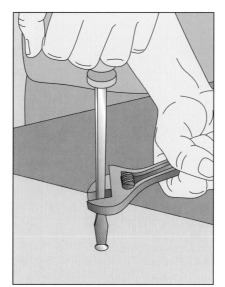

Add force to a screwdriver.

If you need greater turning power, use a screwdriver with a square shank in conjunction with an adjustable wrench. Adjust the wrench so it fits tightly on the screwdriver. Press down on the handle of the screwdriver with the palm of your hand as you turn with the wrench.

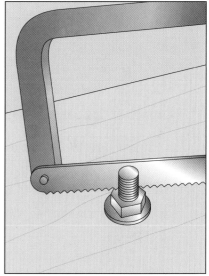

Cut a stubborn nut.

Rusty or damaged bolt threads make it hard to remove a nut. You can solve the problem quickly with a hacksaw. Align the saw blade so it rubs against the threads and cut down through the nut. You will cut off about one-third of the nut. Once you have done this, it will be easy to knock the nut loose or unscrew it.

GLUING AND CLAMPING

A joint will be stronger if you use glue in addition to nails or screws. For some projects that do not require great strength, glue alone will be enough.

Use contact cement to attach wood veneers or plastic laminates to wood surfaces. Apply the cement to both surfaces and let them dry. Align the parts precisely before you join them—the first bond is permanent (see page 61). Use paneling adhesives to attach sheet goods to walls (see page 106). For interior projects, use carpenter's glue with aliphatic resin. This is superior to standard white glue because it sets up faster, resists heat and moisture better, and is stronger. For the glue to work, however, the pieces must be clamped together firmly until the glue sets.

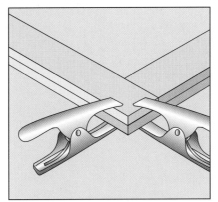

Use speedy squeeze clamps.
For light work, these are the easiest clamps to use. Apply glue to both pieces and place them together in correct alignment. Squeeze the clamp handles to spread the jaws. When you release the handles, the springs will clamp the work together. You may want to have several sizes of these inexpensive clamps on hand.

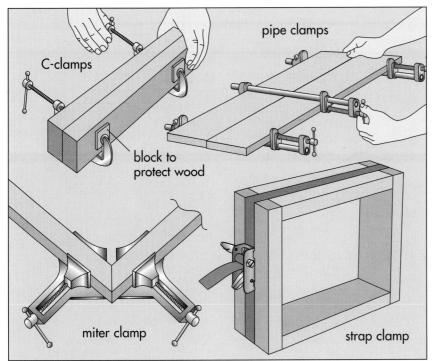

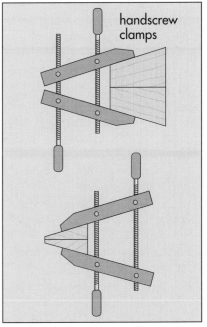

Use the right clamp for the job.
C-clamps are inexpensive and work well when the pieces are not too wide. Use blocks of wood to keep the clamps from marring the boards. For miter joints, use **miter clamps** that hold the boards at a 90-degree angle. For large projects, use **pipe clamps**. You should alternate them to prevent buckling. A **strap clamp** works well for cabinetry projects. It will clamp several joints at once and will not mar the wood.

Use handscrew clamps for angles.
These clamps work well for cabinetmaking and other woodworking projects. Because their jaws are made of wood, you don't have to worry about marring your project. Adjust the clamp to almost any size or angle by simply turning the two handscrews.

CAULKING AND APPLYING MASTIC

It takes practice before you can lay down a clean-looking bead of caulk. Practice on scrap materials or start in an inconspicuous area before you caulk an area that is highly visible.

Choose among a wide variety of adhesives that are designed for particular jobs (see the chart, *below right*). When working with adhesives, be careful to apply the material smoothly and evenly, so the piece will adhere uniformly. Avoid applying too much adhesive; cleaning up messes can take longer than the actual job.

YOU'LL NEED

TIME: About 20 minutes to caulk around a bathtub or countertop; 10 to 30 minutes to adhere laminate or paneling.
SKILLS: Smooth, steady control.
TOOLS: Utility knife, caulking gun, notched trowel.

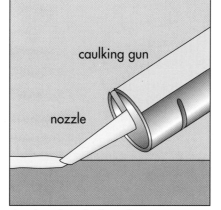

Apply a bead of caulk.
Make sure the joint to be caulked is free of dirt and grease and there are no gaps wider than your bead of caulk. Snip the nozzle of the caulk tube at about a 45-degree angle. The closer to the tip you cut, the smaller the bead will be. You may need to puncture the inside seal with a long nail. Squeeze the handle until caulk starts coming out; move smoothly to apply an even bead.

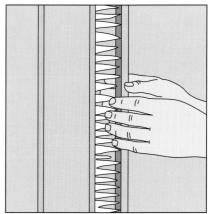

Attach paneling with adhesive.
To attach paneling to walls, apply a bead of adhesive on either the wall or the back of the panel. Use a notched trowel or make a squiggle pattern using a caulking gun. Press the panel against the wall, then pull it out slightly. Wait for a few minutes for the adhesive to get tacky (the manufacturer's instructions will tell you how long), then press the materials together again.

Apply with a notched trowel.
For a smooth, even application, use a notched trowel to apply adhesives. Check the adhesive container for the type and size of notches the trowel should have. Apply the adhesive with the trowel held nearly parallel to the surface to make sure it sticks. Tilt the trowel up at about a 45-degree angle and press firmly as you spread the adhesive.

SELECTING ADHESIVES

Adhesive Type	Primary Use	Holding Power	Moisture-Resistance	Set/Cure Time	Type of Applicator
Contact cement	Applying wood veneer and plastic laminate.	Excellent	Excellent	Must dry first/ 1–2 days	Brush, notched trowel, or paint roller
Epoxy adhesive	Bonding almost any materials. Must mix the parts.	Excellent	Excellent	30 minutes/ 1–10 hours	Throwaway brush or flat stick
Panel adhesive	Attaching drywall or paneling to walls.	Good	Good	1 hour/ 24 hours	Caulk tube or notched trowel
Carpenter's glue	Bonding wood together for small projects.	Good	Fair	30 minutes/ 24 hours	Squeeze-type container
Cyanoacrylate (superglue)	Bonding small items of most any material.	Good	Fair	1–2 minutes/ 24 hours	Squeeze tube

APPLYING LAMINATE

Plastic laminate comes in a variety of colors, patterns, and textures. With practice and the right tools, you can lay down laminate as well, if not as quickly, as a professional.

Be sure that the surface to which you are attaching the laminate is straight, smooth, and supported so it will not flex. New particleboard works best, although laminate also can be applied to plywood and old laminate.

YOU'LL NEED

TIME: About half a day to cover a couple of straightforward countertops.

SKILLS: Accurate measuring and cutting, smooth application of cement, use of a router.

TOOLS: Circular saw or carbide-tipped knife; brush, paint roller, or notched trowel; roller; router, file, or sanding block.

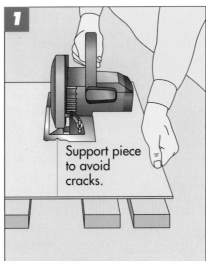

1. Cut the laminate.

Cut the laminate so it is about ½ inch larger than the surface in both directions; you'll trim it exactly after it is installed. Cut it with a circular saw or score its face with a carbide-tipped knife. Cut with the face up if you are using a tablesaw or with the face down if you are using a circular saw.

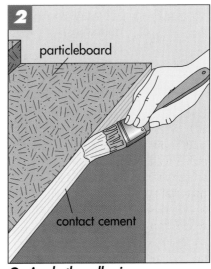

2. Apply the adhesive.

Choose professional-grade contact cement, which costs a bit more than the homeowner-type cement. Spread it evenly on the back of the laminate and the base surface, using a brush, paint roller, or a notched trowel. Allow both surfaces to dry completely before adhering.

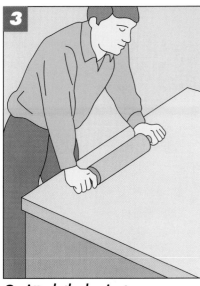

3. Attach the laminate.

Cover the surface with brown wrapping paper and position the laminate on top. When the laminate is exactly where you want it, carefully pull out the paper. Roll the entire surface with a rolling pin, starting in the middle and working outward.

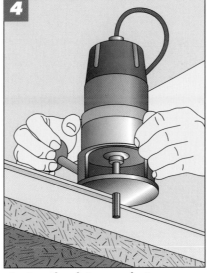

4. Attach edging, and trim.

Attach the edging pieces so they butt tightly against the underside of the top laminate piece. To finish the project, trim the overhanging edges of laminate with a router, file, or sanding block. Take care not to crack the laminate or lift it up as you work.

TOOLS TO USE

■ For the best results, use a router with a special laminate edging bit. This will give you smooth, professional-looking edges that you can't get with a sanding block, rasp, or file. Experiment with the router on scrap pieces to get the depth of the bit set right; if it is too deep, you will cut away too much and ruin the project.

■ For small jobs or for areas where the router can't reach, use a sanding block or a rasp. Work slowly. If you sand away too much laminate, there is no way to fix it.

MAKING SIMPLE, STRONG JOINTS

Strong, good-looking wood joints are essential to all carpentry and woodworking projects. Here are some of the simplest and strongest joinery methods. Each of these joints can be made with hand tools, but if you have shop tools, such as a tablesaw or power miter saw, the job will go faster and the joint will be tighter. None of them requires cabinetmaking expertise.

You'll need to hone your measuring, cutting, and fastening skills to make neat, sturdy joints. See pages 28–59 for a review of the basic techniques.

All of the joints shown on this page are **butt joints**—two square-cut pieces joined together by positioning the end of one member against the face or edge of another member. A butt joint can be fastened with nails or screws only. It will be stronger, however, if reinforced with corner braces, T-plates, angle brackets, dowels, a plywood gusset, or a wood block.

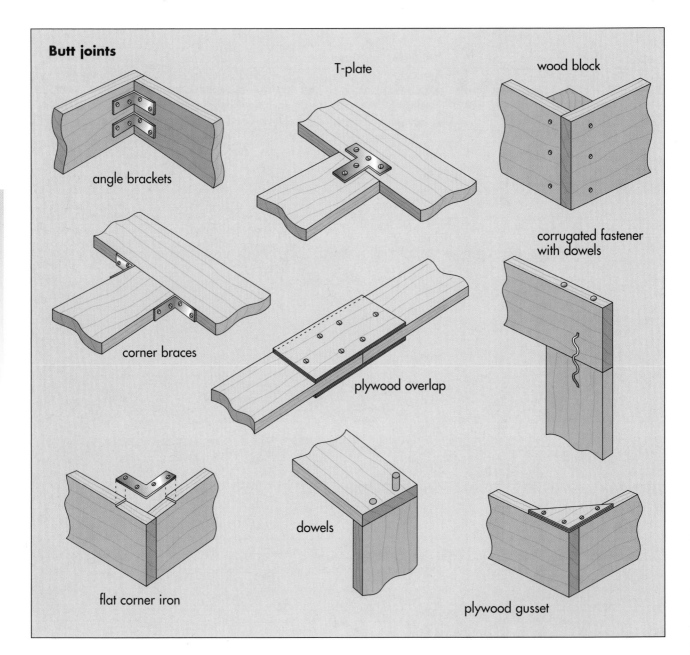

Butt joints

angle brackets

T-plate

wood block

corrugated fastener with dowels

corner braces

plywood overlap

flat corner iron

dowels

plywood gusset

Lap joints are stronger than butt joints and often look better, as well. To make an **overlap joint,** simply lay one of the members on top of the other and nail or screw it in place. For a **full-lap joint,** cut a notch into one member that is as deep as the second piece is thick. Clamp and glue the two pieces together, adding fasteners if you prefer. The **half-lap joint** is the strongest joint (see page 64).

Dado joints are attractive and strong, but are difficult to make.

A **stopped dado** has the strength of a dado and hides the joinery (see page 64).

For a finished-looking corner, make a **miter joint.** Cut the pieces at the same angle (usually 45 degrees), then glue the joint and drive in finishing nails.

A **biscuit joint** also is strong and has the advantage of being completely hidden, To make it, however, requires a biscuit joiner power tool (see page 65).

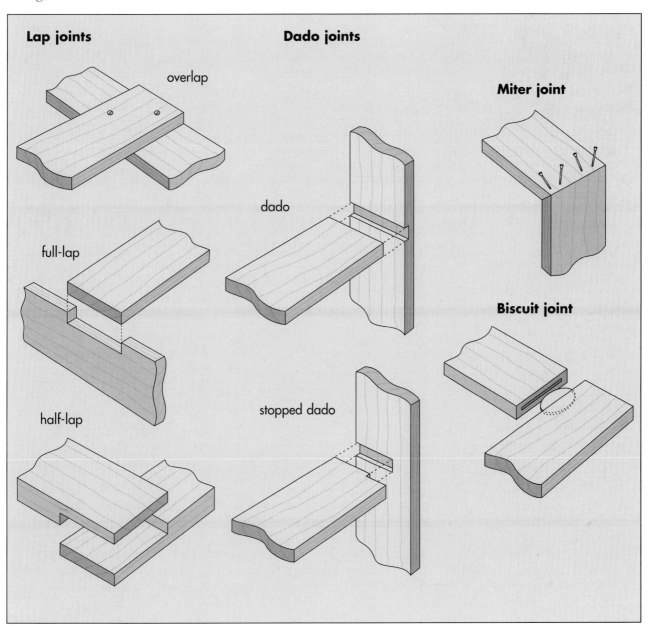

Lap joints — overlap, full-lap, half-lap

Dado joints — dado, stopped dado

Miter joint

Biscuit joint

MAKING A HALF-LAP OR DADO JOINT

Shelves and other wooden structures made with half-lap or dado joints are clearly a cut above those made with butt or even miter joints. Half-laps and dadoes are the stuff of cabinetry rather than carpentry. However, these strong joints don't require a talent for fine woodworking skills, just some skill with basic marking, cutting, and chiseling. Both joints require precise notches. Use sharp saw blades and chisels. To hone your notching skills, practice on a scrap piece of lumber.

YOU'LL NEED

TIME: Allow about 1 hour to make two joints.
SKILLS: Precise marking, cutting, and chiseling skills.
TOOLS: Circular, table, or radial-arm saw; square; chisel.

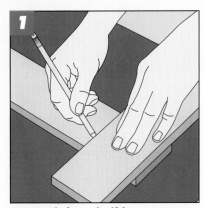

1. Mark for a half-lap joint ...
Overlap the pieces where you want the half-lap joint. You may want to use clamps. Mark for the notches by running a sharp pencil or a knife along the edge of the board. Mark for the notch on the second board using the same method. Or, wait until the first notch has been cut so you can set it over the second board before making your marks.

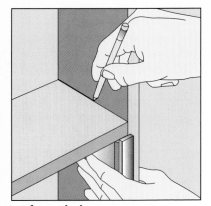

or for a dado.
Hold one piece up against the piece that will be notched. Mark along both sides with a sharp pencil or a knife. Or, mark a perpendicular line and use a scrap piece as a spacer to mark the second line. If you are sure of your skills, you can use a ruler or tape measure to mark for both sides of the notch.

2. Cut a series of kerfs ...
For a half-lap joint, set your saw blade so it cuts exactly halfway through the board. For a dado joint, set the blade to cut one-third of the way through. Keeping the blade on the inside of the notch at all times, make the two outside cuts, then make a series of cuts about ³/₈ inch apart in the area between.

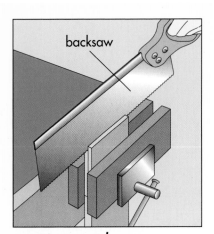

or cut out a notch.
If your cut falls at the end of the board (whether for a half-lap or a dado joint), you simply can cut out a notch. Set your power saw to cut a kerf where the notch will end. Taking care to keep the blade square on both sides, use a backsaw to cut into the end of the board until the blade reaches the first kerf.

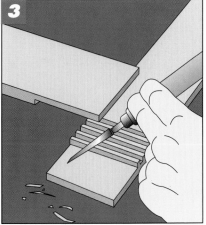

3. Clean out and join.
Using a chisel with its beveled surface down, clean remaining wood out of the notch. Make sure the visible edges are straight and there are no bumps in the middle of the notch. Dry-fit the pieces to make sure they are tight. Apply carpenter's glue, clamp, and fasten with nails or screws.

FASTENING WITH DOWELS

A dowel joint is not impressive-looking like a half-lap or dado joint, but it is strong. Making a dowel joint requires no special tools, but there are two difficulties: You must hold the boards square as you work and you must hold the drill as straight as possible to keep from poking a hole through the edge or side of a board. Work on a flat surface to keep the face of the boards even. If possible, clamp the boards together before adding the dowels.

YOU'LL NEED

TIME: 1 hour to make two dowel joints.
SKILLS: Good drilling skills.
TOOLS: Drill with an extra-long bit, backsaw, hammer.

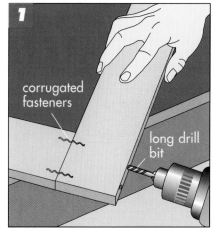

1. Temporarily join and drill.
Position the boards the way you want them and join them temporarily with fasteners or clamps. If you use fasteners, make sure they will not be in the way of the dowels. Square up the corner and drill holes for the dowels.

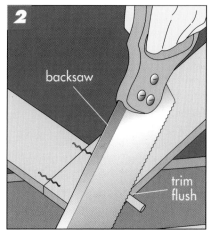

2. Drive the dowels and trim off.
Squirt carpenter's glue into the drill holes and insert the dowels. Tap them all the way in and clean away excess glue. Cut off the dowels as flush to the board as possible without scratching the edge. Sand the remainder smooth.

FASTENING WITH A BISCUIT JOINER

With this tool, you can create neat, sturdy joints with ease. Biscuit fasteners are oval-shaped pieces of plywood that fit invisibly into incisions inside the joint. You can use a biscuit joiner to fasten two boards on edge, join ¾-inch or thicker edging to plywood, or make butt or miter joints. Be sure you hold the tool with its base perfectly flat against the board as you make the cuts. If you will be using more than three or four biscuits on a joint, work fast and have a helper on hand.

YOU'LL NEED

TIME: About 30 minutes to make two joints with eight biscuits.
SKILLS: Use of power tools, ability to align the tool and hold it flat.
TOOLS: Biscuit joiner, hammer, clamps, square.

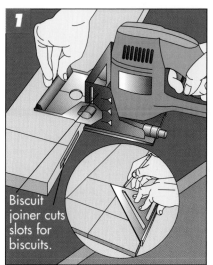

1. Mark and cut.
Position the boards as you want them joined. For every place you want to install a biscuit, mark a line running from one board to the other (see inset). Set the tool to the correct depth for the size biscuit you're using. Hold the tool flat against the board as you make each incision.

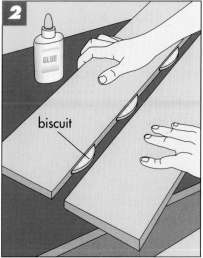

2. Glue, join, and clamp.
After dry-fitting the boards with the biscuits in place, squirt a little carpenter's glue into each incision. Set the biscuits into the incisions and tap the second board into place, sliding the biscuits into their respective slots. Check that the joint is tight and clamp. Wipe away excess glue and allow to dry.

SHAPING AND PLANING

Beveling edges and corners, planing down doors, trueing edges and ends of lumber—most carpentry projects include at least one of these shaping tasks. Three types of tools work best for shaping wood surfaces: planes, surface-forming tools, and rasps or wood files. With practice and a clean, sharp tool, shaping can be a pleasure rather than a chore.

However, even the sharpest shaping tools are no match for a board that's badly twisted, bowed, cupped, or warped (see page 16). Always inspect your material for flaws and select only the stock suitable for the job. Don't assume you can shape it up later.

EXPERTS' INSIGHT

SCRIBING A TRUE LINE

■ To straighten out a piece of lumber or a door, you must first draw the line indicating where the piece should end. This is called a true line. A true line is usually straight, but not always. For instance, a door often must be planed to fit an opening that is not straight. To make a true line, scribe it by holding the piece up against the place into which it must fit. Run your pencil along the opening as you mark the piece for planing.

■ When scribing a line, check the angle at which you are holding the pencil and the thickness of the pencil line. Hold the pencil at the same angle at all points along your scribe line or you will cut off too little or too much wood. Decide if you want to cut off all of the pencil mark or just up to the mark.

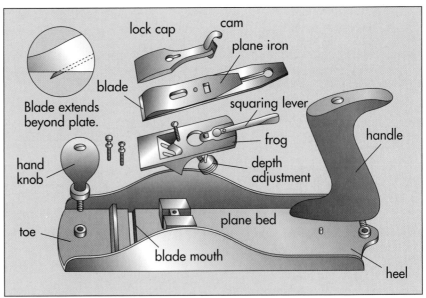

Keep planes in working order.

Various types and sizes of planes are available. Most carpenters use a smoothing plane (shown *above*) or a small block plane (see page 67). To help keep the blade from dulling, lay it on its side when not in use. Retract the blade into the body when storing it. If any parts become rusty, clean them with a little oil and fine steel wool. Adjust the blade so it cuts thin shavings easily; you should not have to fight against the wood.

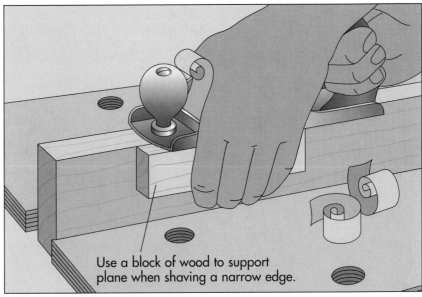

Use a block of wood to support plane when shaving a narrow edge.

Follow general planing rules.

Follow these tips when using a plane or surface-former:

■ It takes both hands to operate the tool, so clamp your work.

■ Plane with the grain.

■ If you get anything but a continuous, even shaving, the blade is dull or adjusted too thick, or you're planing against the grain.

■ To avoid nicking corners, apply pressure to the knob of the tool at the beginning of your cut and to its heel at the end of the cut.

■ When planing a narrow edge, grip a square-cornered block of wood against the bottom of the plane as you work.

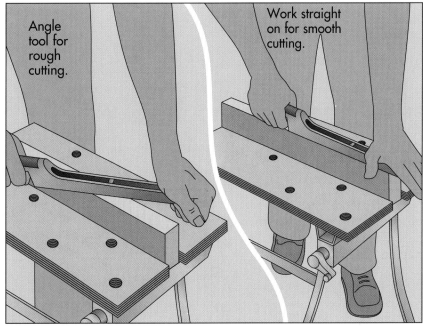

Shape with surface-forming tools.
Surface-forming tools, also known as sure-form tools, come in a variety of sizes and shapes. The one shown, *above*, works much like a plane. You cannot adjust the depth of the cut and it will not produce as smooth a cut as a plane, but it is easy to use.

You can regulate the cut by the way you position the tool against the material. For rough-cutting, hold the tool at a 45-degree angle to the work as you push it. For a smoother result, hold the tool parallel to the board's edge.

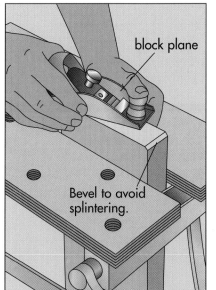

Shape end grain with a block.
As long as you're shaping wood parallel to the grain, planing will go smoothly. But when you need to shape the end grain, you will be working at a 90-degree angle to the grain. A small block plane works best on end grain. Bevel the

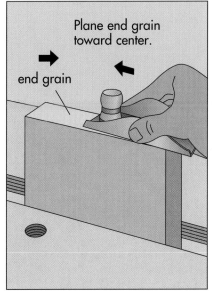

corners first, with the bottom of the bevel at the final cut line. For narrow stock, just plane in one direction. For wider material, shave from each end of the board toward the center. Finish the job by shaving off the hump that remains in the middle.

TOOLS TO USE

POWER PLANER AND BELT SANDER

■ If you have a lot of planing to do, buy a power planer. The depth is easy to adjust, and as long as you hold the base flat against the surface, you will get a smooth cut with little effort. Be sure to use carbide-tipped blades, or you will have to change them often.

■ If you can work carefully, a belt sander shaves material, especially softwoods, with relative ease. Start with a coarse sandpaper. Hold the sanding belt flat to the surface; you'll make gouges if you tip the tool. Once you have taken off almost as much material as you need to, switch to a smoother paper.

SANDING

Once you've taken the time to cut and assemble your project, don't skimp when it comes to the final steps. Do a thorough job of sanding, so the wood will be well prepared for its final finish. Don't expect stain, varnish, or paint to smooth out the surface for you. They will only follow the contours of the wood, and often will accentuate, rather than hide, imperfections. Unless you are using a belt sander with a rough abrasive, don't expect sanding to remove more than ⅛ inch of material; shape or plane instead (see pages 66–67).

CAUTION!
Particularly when sanding with power tools, wear a face mask. To avoid difficult cleanup later, seal the room.

Use a belt sander for rough work.
Use this tool only on rough surfaces and only if you are sure of yourself; it is easy to make gouges if you tip the tool or if you rest it in one spot too long. Always run the sander with the grain, never against it. Don't apply pressure as you work; just let the weight of the sander do the work.

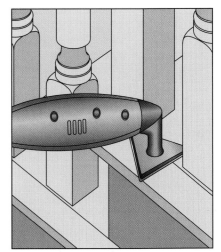

Use a detail sander in tight spots.
For awkward areas, a detail sander can spare you hours of finger-throbbing work. Sanding pads are self-adhesive; just lift one off and put the next one on. Proceed carefully. A detail sander works with an oscillating action. Because it concentrates on such a small area, it takes off material quickly.

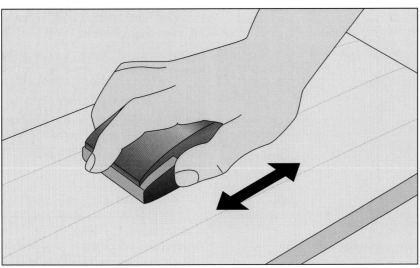

Hand-sand with a block.
Except in hard-to-reach areas, never use abrasive sheets alone—always use some sort of sanding block, either store-bought or improvised. Sanding with a block is less tiring and produces more uniform results.

Tear abrasive sheets to size, rather than cutting them, or you will dull your knife blade quickly.

Check that the bottom of your block is clean and smooth. Any debris can tear the paper and mar your work.

Sand only in the direction of the wood grain. Sanding across the grain or in a circular motion can leave hard-to-remove lines. Don't exert a lot of pressure. If you're using the right grade of paper, light strokes are all you'll need.

EXPERTS' INSIGHT

SAND THREE TIMES
■ Take the time and trouble to sand three times, using progressively finer sandpaper. The wood surface may feel smooth after your first and second sandings, but it will get smoother as you move on to finer-grit sandpapers. A common progression is to start with 80-grit paper, then proceed to 120-, 180-, and possibly even 240-grit abrasives. Clean dust from the wood between sandings.
■ If you can't sand out a stain or discoloration, apply a small amount of laundry bleach to the stain. Try several applications until you get the right color. Dry before sanding it again.

Use ingenuity for tight spots.

When smoothing wood in tight quarters or in unusual situations, special tools can help. Consider buying or renting a detail sander (see page 68) or a contour sanding attachment for your drill.

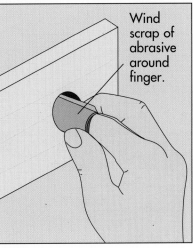

Often, however, you can get the job done with a sheet of abrasive and a little ingenuity, as these three examples show.

To sand two surfaces where they meet at an inside corner, wrap a creased sheet of abrasive

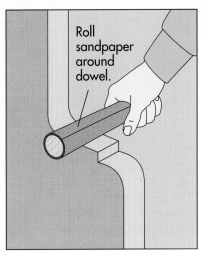

around a sharp-cornered block. To smooth inside edges of bored holes and small cutouts, wrap abrasive around your finger or a small round object. For sanding outside curves, wrap a sheet of abrasive around a dowel.

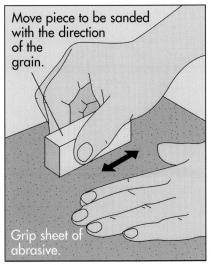

Sand a small piece.

When you need to smooth the surface of a small item, sand it on a full sheet of abrasive held flat with your free hand. This keeps the surface of the piece even and flat. If the abrasive fills with dust, wipe it with a clean cloth or give it a few slaps against your bench.

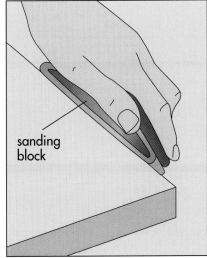

Round off edges.

Because wood edges are susceptible to nicks and splinters, it is a good idea to blunt them with a light sanding. Hold the sanding block at an angle; use gentle pressure combined with a rocking motion. A molded rubber sanding block like the one shown, *above,* is ideal for this purpose because its base gives slightly.

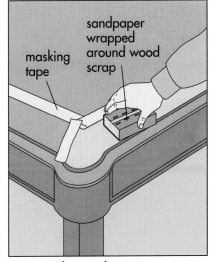

Protect edges with tape.

Sometimes you'll want to sand one surface without scratching an adjoining surface. To do this, protect the surface you don't want sanded with masking tape. Affix the tape carefully, making sure it is stuck down tightly at all points. Watch closely as you sand and immediately replace any tape that gets ripped or damaged.

FILLING AND FINISHING

Paint, stain, or clear finishes rarely cover up imperfections in wood. Often, they make things look worse rather than better. It pays to prepare your wood carefully before you add a finish.

Fill in holes with wood filler and sand the surface smooth. If you're applying a clear finish, limit your use of putty to small spots; even putty that is made to accept stain never quite looks like real wood. Even if you're going to paint the surface, cover exposed plywood edges. They soak up paint like a sponge and will look rough no matter how many coats of paint you apply to them.

Once the wood surface is prepared, match your paint or clear finish to the intended use of your project. See chart on *page 71* for selecting finishes.

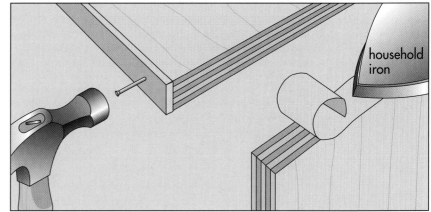

Cover plywood edges.
To conceal a plywood edge, cut a thin piece of molding to fit, apply carpenter's glue to the edge, and fasten the molding with brads (small finishing nails). You also can cover an edge with wood veneer tape. Buy tape that is wider than the thickness of the material and matches its surface. Cut the tape with scissors, leaving at least 1/4 inch extra on all edges. Position iron-on tape carefully, so it covers the edge along the entire length. Apply even, steady pressure with a household iron set on high. Use contact cement to apply non-iron-on veneer. Trim the edges with a sharp knife, then sand the corners lightly.

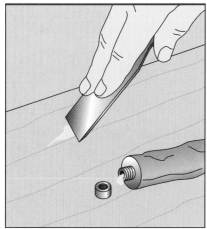

Fill in nail and screw holes.
For small holes, use a dough-type wood filler. Apply filler either before or after staining; experiment to find out which looks best. Begin by tamping a small amount of the filler into the hole with your thumb. Smooth it with a putty knife. Wipe away the excess with a rag dampened with water or mineral spirits, depending on the type of putty (check manufacturer's directions).

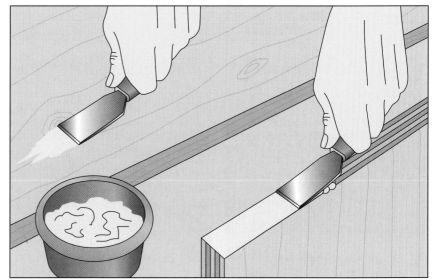

Fill in large areas.
If you're going to paint the entire surface of a project, water-mix putty excels at filling shallow depressions over a large surface area. The putty sets up quickly, so don't mix more than you can use in 10 minutes. To fill cracks around a knot, mix the putty to a pastelike consistency and force it into all the cracks with a putty knife. Feather out the patch to the surrounding wood. To fill edges of plywood or the end grain of boards, mix the putty to a thinner consistency. Sand and apply a second coat if necessary. For deep holes, you may have to apply two layers to allow for any shrinkage of the putty.

SELECTING CLEAR FINISHES

Type	Characteristics	Application and Drying Time
Natural-resin varnish	Resists scratches, scuffs. Spar varnish good outdoors.	Use varnish brush or cheesecloth pad. Dries in 24–36 hours. In humid weather, allow 36 hours.
Polyurethane varnish	Mar-resistant, durable, remains clear.	Use natural-bristle brush, roller, or spray. Let dry 1–2 hours; 12 hours between coats.
Two-part epoxy varnish	High resistance to scuffs and mars. Ideal for floors.	Use brush. Check directions if coating wood filler. First coat dries in 3 hours; second in 5–8 hours.
Shellac	Easily damaged by water. Clear or pigmented.	Use small brush with chiseled tip. Thin with alcohol or recommended solvent. Dries in about 2 hours.
Lacquer	Fast-drying. Ideal for furniture.	Best sprayed in many thin coats. Let last coat dry 48–60 hours, then rub with fine steel wool or hard wax.
Resin oil	Soaks into and hardens grain. Resists scratches.	Usually hand-rubbed in 2–3 coats. Needs 8–12 hours to dry.

Apply penetrating stain.
Apply stain with a brush and wait for a few minutes. The heavier the application and the longer you wait, the deeper the color. Wipe with a clean rag, taking care to make the color even throughout the piece. To make it darker, apply a second coat. If it is too dark, rub with a cloth moistened with the recommended thinner.

Begin with strokes across the grain.

Finish with long strokes with the grain.

Paint correctly for a smooth look.
Painting with a brush may seem like a simple task, but here are a few tips to keep in mind. Begin applying paint to wood surfaces with short strokes across the wood grain, laying down paint in both directions. Don't bear down too hard on the bristles.

Finish painting with longer, sweeping strokes in one direction only—this time with the wood grain. Use just the tips of the bristles to smooth out the paint.

EXPERTS' INSIGHT

ANTIQUING
■ If you have old furniture or cabinets that are worn or marred, you can avoid all the work of stripping, sanding, and refinishing them by emphasizing the wood's imperfections.

■ If you are new to this process, buy an antiquing kit, which usually includes base and finish coating materials and brushes and applicators. Choose from a variety of finishes: marbleized, distressed, spattered, stippled, crumpled, and others.

■ Remove dirt and wax from the surface, apply the base coat, and let it dry. After sanding, apply a finish coat quickly. Wipe it to achieve the desired finish. Allow it to dry for 48 hours and add a clear, protective finish.

INSTALLING MOLDING

Installing molding to finish off a project can be the most gratifying part of the job. Although it's easier than you might expect, installing molding takes some practice. Start installing molding in an area of the room where it will be the least visible. You'll soon surprise yourself with your speed and neat joinery. The most common mistake is to cut a miter in the wrong direction. Whenever possible, mark pieces clearly, not only for length, but also for the direction of cut.

YOU'LL NEED

TIME: About 10 minutes per piece of molding.
SKILLS: Precise measuring and cutting, figuring out the direction of cuts, nailing.
TOOLS: Tape measure, miter box and backsaw or power miter saw, coping saw, hammer, nail set.

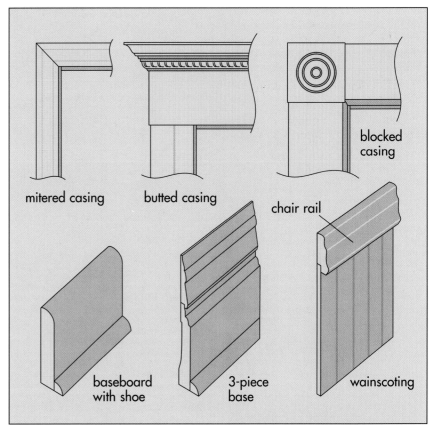

mitered casing   butted casing   blocked casing

chair rail

baseboard with shoe   3-piece base   wainscoting

EXPERTS' INSIGHT

BUYING MOLDING

Molding can be expensive, so determine exactly how many pieces of each size you need. On a piece of paper, make columns for each size—8 feet, 10 feet, 12 feet, etc. As you measure for individual pieces, tally how many you need under each column. If you have an old house, you may need moldings that are not made any longer. A lumberyard with a mill or a millwork company can make replicas. If the price is too high or you need only a small piece of molding, you can make a reasonable facsimile using a router, tablesaw, radial-arm saw, and belt sander.

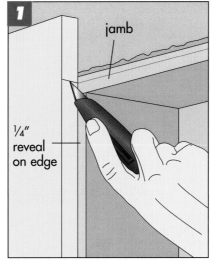

jamb

¼" reveal on edge

1. Measure and mark precisely.
Whenever possible, hold a piece of molding in place and mark it with a knife, rather than using a tape measure. For window and door casings, take into account the ¼-inch reveal on the edge of the jamb. As a guide, use a compass set to ¼ inch to mark the reveal on the jamb.

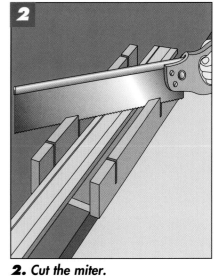

2. Cut the miter.
Sight down the blade of the saw and slide the molding until the saw will cut just to the scrap side of your mark. Hold the molding against the back of the miter box, as shown *above*. Grasp it tightly so it will not slide as you cut it. As an alternative, use a power miter saw or radial-arm saw (see page 50).

INSTALLING BASE MOLDING

Install door and window casing and other vertical molding before you install molding at the bottom of your walls. Choose from ranch or colonial base molding or use a three-piece base for a traditional look (see page 72). It is best to add a quarter round or base shoe as well. These types bend easily with variations in the flooring and buffer scuffs from vacuum cleaners.

You may be tempted simply to miter-cut pieces for inside corners. This often leads to unsightly gaps and misaligned joints because the corners are almost never true 90-degree angles. Instead, cut the first piece to length with a regular 90-degree cut and cope-cut the second piece (see page 41).

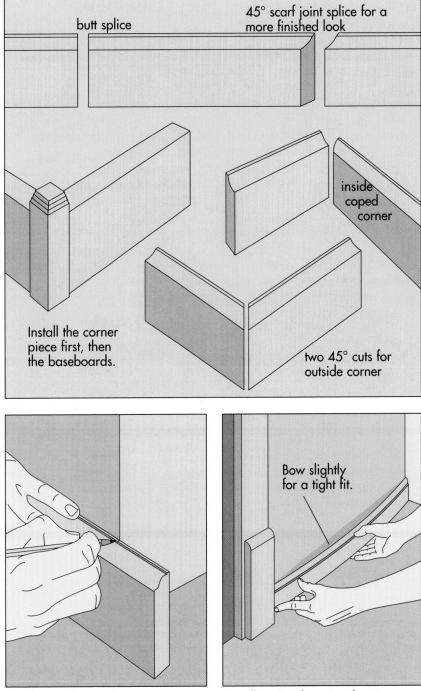

butt splice

45° scarf joint splice for a more finished look

inside coped corner

Install the corner piece first, then the baseboards.

two 45° cuts for outside corner

ACHIEVING THAT PROFESSIONAL LOOK

■ Avoid splits. Thin stock, such as often is used for baseboard molding, is prone to splitting and cracking. Don't take chances. Wherever you will be driving a nail within 3 inches of the edge of a piece, drill a pilot hole. You may be able to simply attach a short piece of molding with construction adhesive.

■ Don't overnail. The most common mistake amateurs make when installing moldings is to put in too many nails. Drive in only as many as you need to hold the piece firmly flush against the wall.

■ Stain first, but paint second. If you will be staining molding, do it before you install it. If you will be painting, install the molding first, then paint.

Mark outside corners.
As with all molding, for greater accuracy, hold and mark the pieces in place wherever possible (see page 30). For an outside corner, butt one end of the molding in place, allowing the other to extend past the corner. Make the mark exactly even with the corner.

Bow slightly for a tight fit.

Install an inside-to-inside piece.
Mark and cut the piece about 1/16 inch longer than the space. If you are butting against a piece of casing, make sure the casing is well-secured so it does not move when you press against it. Install the baseboard by bending it into position. This will give you a tight fit on both sides.

INSTALLING CROWN MOLDING

Transform a boxy room with the elegant and softening beauty of crown molding. With more and more molding profiles available, you have plenty of options for adding an attractive finishing touch to your home.

Although installing crown molding takes patience and a few tricks of the trade, homeowners who are comfortable with basic carpentry tools and who have coped molding miters before should have few problems. Careful fitting and refitting are crucial to obtaining a close fit between sections of molding.

When working over your head, a solid working platform makes all the difference. Don't try to do the careful fitting and nailing that crown molding requires while working from a stepladder. Make the job easier on yourself by finding a plank and two sturdy sawhorses to make a platform to stand on while installing the molding. In addition, enlist a coworker to hold the lengths of molding while you measure, position, and fasten them.

Before beginning this challenging project, review marking and measuring techniques (pages 28–29), how to use a miter box (page 38), and nailing techniques (pages 52–53).

YOU'LL NEED
TIME: About 4 hours for a 12×12-foot room
SKILLS: Precise measuring, use of miter box or power miter saw, driving nails.
TOOLS: Deep miter box with backsaw or power miter box, drill, hammer, nail set.

CAUTION!
WHICH SIDE IS UP?
Remember to think upside down as you make miter cuts. Double-check which edge of the crown molding goes up—the difference is subtle.

Money $ Saver

PRACTICE MAKES PERFECT

To avoid expensive mistakes with crown molding, you should hone your mitering and coping skills before you plunge into the job. Ask your local home center or lumber dealer for a 2- or 3-foot scrap of molding similar to the type you plan to use. Practice the steps shown on these pages.

It is particularly important to gain some familiarity with the way molding is cut and coped. The more proficient you are at making overlapping joints, the less likely you are to make costly errors.

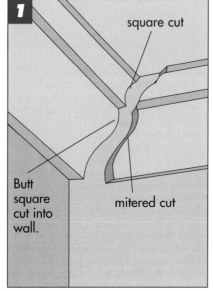

1. Cut the first piece square.
To achieve a mitered look with corners that are seldom perfectly square, run the first piece of crown molding tightly into the corner. Cope-cut the second piece in the shape of the profile of the molding, so it can butt neatly against the face of the first piece.

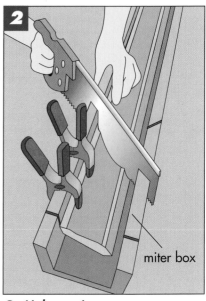

2. Make a miter cut.
Use a deep miter box and a fine-toothed backsaw to make a cut that reveals the profile of the molding. Position the molding so that it is upside down in the miter box. The face of the molding that goes against the ceiling will be on the bottom of the miter box. Remember, for inside corners, the bottom of the crown molding will be the longest edge.

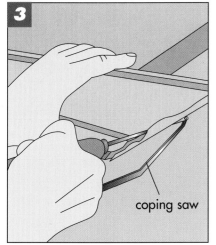

3. Cope the profile.

If the mitered cut is correct, you'll be able to see the profile of the molding. Cut away the excess wood along the back side of the molding with a coping saw. Err on the side of removing too much rather than too little; only the outermost edge of the coped molding will be seen.

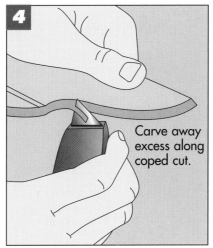

Carve away excess along coped cut.

4. Fine-tune your cut.

Use a utility knife to remove any excess material you missed with the coping saw. Be careful that you do not cut into the exposed face of the molding. Hold the piece in place to test the fit. Take it down and do more carving if necessary.

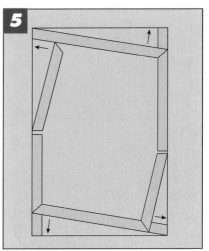

5. Plan each joint.

Map out the job so that one end of each piece of crown molding always will be cut straight and one end will be mitered and coped. Use butt joints for long runs. Save the most visible parts of the job for last, when you've honed your coping skills.

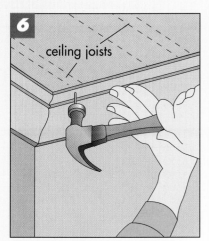

ceiling joists

6. Nail in place ...

If the molding runs perpendicular to the ceiling joists, determine the location of the joists. Drill pilot holes to keep the molding from splitting. As you attach the molding, tack it in place with a few nails. Take a good look at the positioning before completing the nailing.

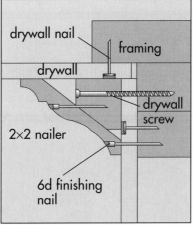

drywall nail

framing

drywall

drywall screw

2×2 nailer

6d finishing nail

or add a nailer.

To provide a solid nailing area where the joists run parallel to the crown molding, cut a beveled face on a 2×2, as shown. Cut the 2×2 to length and screw it to the wall so it's in the corner of the ceiling and the wall. The 2×2 provides a surface, at the proper angle, to which you can nail the molding.

TOOLS TO USE

BE SHARP

The right tools—kept clean and sharp—help make a precise job, such as installing crown molding, easier. Here are some tips:

■ Drop off your saw for professional sharpening well before you begin the job. A sharpened saw provides better control and a cleaner cut, and it makes the job go more pleasantly.

■ Buy new coping-saw blades. They break easily, so have half a dozen on hand.

■ Have plenty of clamps to hold the molding while you cut it. The less you rely on your own holding power, the easier and more accurately you'll be able to make the saw cuts.

PLANNING FOR NEW CABINETS

Sometimes you can remodel old cabinets by painting them, replacing the doors and hardware, or hiring a company that specializes in applying new finishes. Often, however, the best solution is to install new cabinets. With careful planning and modest carpentry skills, you can do this project yourself.

When designing a kitchen, measure your space exactly and map out a wall plan on a piece of graph paper. As you plan, allow an extra inch or so for the width of the stove or refrigerator and for overhead clearance. Make sure that all cabinet doors, as well as those on the dishwasher and range, can open freely.

Many people prefer to have a soffit—a partial wall—coming down from the ceiling to meet the top of the wall cabinets. Building soffits is a lot of work; consider topping off wall cabinets with crown molding instead (see pages 74–75).

Unless you're a real stickler for symmetry, there's no reason to make the wall cabinets the same width as the base cabinets. Your cabinet supply center will have someone to check your design.

As you plan for new cabinets, upgrade the rest of your kitchen as well. With the old cabinets gone, it's an ideal time to add electrical outlets, under-the-cabinet lights, flooring, and new plumbing and to patch and paint your walls.

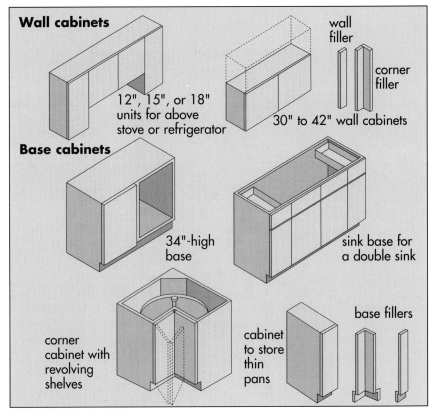

Select from many cabinet types.
Ready-made cabinets come in a limited number of sizes, so chances are you will need to buy filler pieces to make up gaps of 1 to 3 inches here and there. Base cabinets are typically 24 inches deep and 34½ inches tall; once you add the countertop, your surface will be 36 inches high. Wall cabinets are usually 12 inches deep and 30 to 42 inches tall. There are special cabinets designed for corners, to hold sinks, and to go above stoves and refrigerators.

YOU'LL NEED

TIME: 1 day to map out your space, 1 day to install cabinets for a medium-size kitchen.
SKILLS: Measuring, leveling, drilling, driving screws.
TOOLS: Level, tape measure, drill, pry bar, hammer.

EXPERTS' INSIGHT

CHOOSING CABINETS

■ Most manufacturers have several lines of cabinets, each priced according to the quality of materials used in their construction. You can save money by buying cabinets that need assembly or require finishing.
■ Closely inspect cabinets before buying. The doors should swing freely, latch securely, and line up straight. Drawers should glide on two metal tracks. Adjustable hinges are a plus because doors get out of alignment over time.
■ Particleboard and hardboard cabinets often come with hardwood or plastic veneers; once scratched, these are difficult to repair. Screws driven into the particleboard do not hold well, and hinges can come loose.
■ Although more expensive, hardwood is the best choice for doors, frames, and sides. It holds up against abuse and can be repaired. When finished properly, hardwood is easy to care for.

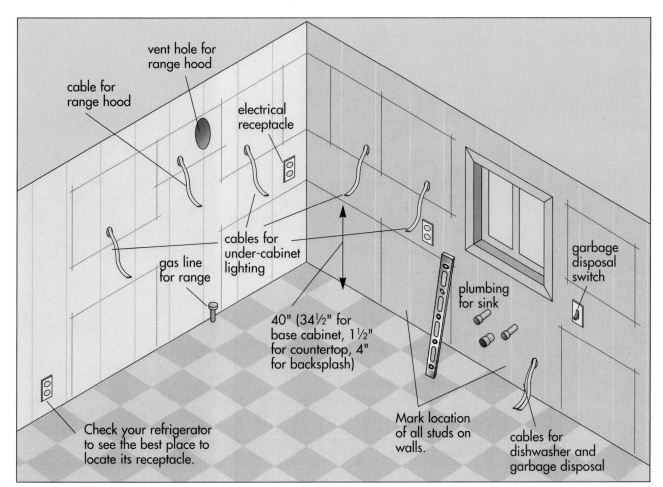

vent hole for range hood

cable for range hood

electrical receptacle

cables for under-cabinet lighting

gas line for range

garbage disposal switch

plumbing for sink

40" (34½" for base cabinet, 1½" for countertop, 4" for backsplash)

Mark location of all studs on walls.

Check your refrigerator to see the best place to locate its receptacle.

cables for dishwasher and garbage disposal

Prepare and lay out walls.

Clear out the old cabinets. Check your floor for level. If it's off by only half an inch or so, you can shim up the base cabinets. If it's way out of level, either level out the floor or plan to have your cabinets somewhat out of level as well, parallel to the floor so the difference will not be noticeable. If you will be installing new flooring, it usually is easiest to do it before you install cabinets. Also, check your walls for plumb. Depending on which way they lean, you may need to move the cabinets or plan on shimming them plumb.

Start at the highest point on the floor (see page 33) and draw outlines of your base cabinets on the wall. Measure up from these lines and draw outlines of your wall cabinets. A standard kitchen countertop is 36 inches high; the bottom of the wall cabinets should be 54 inches above the floor.

Take a good look at your outlines and visualize how your kitchen will look and work. Use old cabinets or pieces of wood of the same dimensions to get a clear idea of how the cabinets will fit into the space. Now, rather than later, is the best time to change your mind about the cabinet configuration you want. You may want to leave more room around a window or give yourself a couple of inches of more traffic space. Be sure that all doors—entry and cabinet—will open freely.

Rough-in the plumbing and complete the electrical work before installing cabinets. Estimate the wattage demand of your lighting and appliances and plan your electrical circuits so they will not be overloaded.

Decide where you want electrical receptacles. Be sure to account for the height of the backsplash (4 inches) as well as the countertop when locating outlets. Ground-fault circuit interrupters (GFCIs) are required for all receptacles within 6 feet of a sink. Run wiring for the dishwasher and garbage disposal as well as switches for lights and the garbage disposal.

Plan for under-cabinet lighting. To install fluorescent fixtures under the cabinets, run cable as shown. Exactly where you poke the cables through the wall depends on how your cabinets are constructed. Or, you can install low-voltage halogen lighting after the cabinets are installed.

Buy the range hood and find out where the exhaust hole should go in your wall. Cut the hole and install the ductwork.

Patch the portions of the walls that will show after the cabinets are installed and paint them or hang wallpaper. Make light pencil marks on the walls showing the location of your studs.

INSTALLING WALL CABINETS

It's easier to install wall cabinets before base cabinets because you'll have more room to work and lift the cabinets into position. If you do install the base cabinets first, protect them with drop cloths or cardboard while working on the wall cabinets. If you are installing under-cabinet lighting, you may need to drill holes in the wall cabinets for the cable, depending on how the cabinets are constructed. Walls that are not plumb can affect the fit of your cabinets; check for plumb before beginning. Always enlist a helper when installing wall cabinets.

YOU'LL NEED

TIME: 2 to 3 hours for a group of six standard cabinets.
SKILLS: Leveling, drilling, driving screws, shimming.
TOOLS: Level, ruler, drill, clamps, screwdriver bit.

CAUTION!

FASTEN THE CABINETS SECURELY

Wall cabinets do not rest on the floor. All that holds them up are screws driven into the wall. Stacks of plates and canned goods can add up to some extra-heavy loads. Make sure every cabinet is securely anchored to the wall. Fasteners driven into drywall or plaster alone will not do the job. Only screws that are embedded at least 1 inch into wall studs will support fully loaded cabinets.

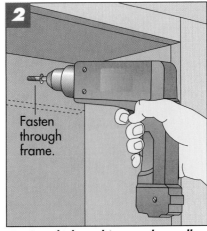

54 inches from floor (18" above top of countertop, which is 36" above floor)

1. Attach a temporary ledger.
To ensure that the cabinets align with each other, secure a straight board with its top edge at the point where you want the bottom of your cabinets to be, usually 54 inches above the floor (18 inches above the countertop). Alternatively, make a 2×4 frame of the appropriate height and rest the cabinets on top of it until they are fastened to the wall.

2. Attach the cabinet to the wall.
If the cabinet is heavy, remove shelves and doors to make it manageable. With a helper, hold the first cabinet in place and check it for plumb. Slip in shims as necessary, and drive screws through the top and bottom framing pieces and into each wall stud. For screw heads that will remain visible, use finish washers. Some manufacturers supply plastic screw-head covers.

Fasten through frame.

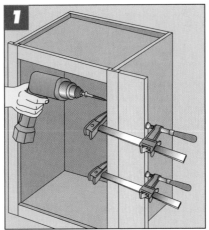

1. Install a spacer at a corner.
In most situations, join wall cabinets together as with base cabinets (see page 79). Spacers can be easily disguised in corners. Begin by attaching the spacer to the cabinet. Rip the spacer to the correct width, clamp it in place, drill and countersink pilot holes, and drive in three screws. Remove the clamps.

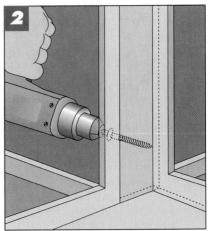

2. Fasten to the next cabinet.
It usually is best not to cover any part of a cabinet frame or you will have trouble closing cabinet doors. In corners, attach the cabinets by drilling and countersinking pilot holes through the spacer. Drive in screws through the spacer and into the frame of the next cabinet.

INSTALLING BASE CABINETS

Find the highest point of your floor by using a level and 2×4 (see page 33). Start at that point; you can shim cabinets up but not down. As you work, take care not to damage the cabinets with your tools. Use screws (most likely supplied by the manufacturer), never nails. If a baseboard or other piece of molding is in the way, remove it and cut it; don't cut the cabinet to fit the molding. If you installed the wall cabinets first, watch your head as you work on the base cabinets.

YOU'LL NEED

TIME: 4 to 6 hours for a medium-size kitchen.
SKILLS: Leveling and plumbing, drilling and driving screws, shimming, clamping.
TOOLS: Level, hammer, drill, screwdriver bit, pry bar, clamps.

Check for level at side and front.

1. Check for level.
Starting at the highest point of the floor, set the first cabinet in place. Check to see that the cabinet is level from front to back as well as from side to side. As a double-check, see if the framing is plumb. Shim the bottom of the cabinet if necessary and recheck that the cabinet is level.

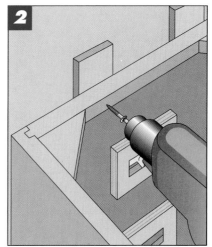

2. Attach cabinet to the wall.
Drill pilot holes and drive in screws through the cabinet framing (not the thin plywood backing) and into wall studs. Wherever the framing is not tight against the wall, use shims to keep the cabinet plumb. Recheck the cabinet for level in both directions before moving on to the next unit.

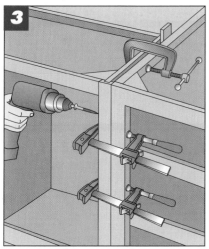

3. Join cabinets together.
To ensure tight, even joints between the cabinets, clamp them in place before fastening. Make sure they are flush with each other, not only along their faces, but also at the top. Drill pilot holes and countersink them (see page 46), then drive in screws to hold the units together firmly. Attach the cabinet to the wall as you did the first one.

toekick   finishing nail

4. Install toekicks or base.
If you have to shim the cabinets, there might be an unsightly gap between the base and the floor. If the toekick was preinstalled, remove it by gently prying it off. Reinstall it flush to the floor. Any gap along the top of the toekick will be hidden. If the toekick was not preinstalled, simply nail it flush to the floor. You also can put a vinyl cove base over the toekick.

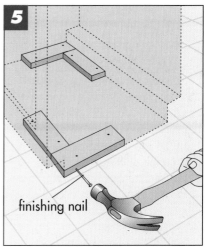

finishing nail

5. Supply backing for an island.
When installing a cabinet that does not sit against a wall (for example, an island unit), you must install a nailing surface on the floor. Turn the cabinet upside down and measure its inside dimensions. Attach pieces of 2×4 to the floor so the cabinet just fits over them. Slip the cabinet into place and attach it to the 2×4s with finishing nails.

INSTALLING COUNTERTOPS

Countertops covered with plastic laminate are fairly durable and economical; thus, they are the most common surfacing choice for base cabinets (see below for other options). If your layout is straightforward, you can buy a ready-made, post-form top, which has a curved front lip and a backsplash. Or, you can laminate or order your own square-edged top. Recognize your limits, however. If your walls are more than ⅜ inch out of square or the situation entails a complicated configuration, call in a countertop professional.

YOU'LL NEED

TIME: 2 to 3 hours to scribe-cut and install a medium-size top.
SKILLS: Careful measuring and cutting, scribing, fastening.
TOOLS: Circular saw and/or sabersaw, belt sander, wrenches, iron, drill.

ALTERNATIVE COUNTERTOP MATERIALS

■ Solid granite countertops are expensive, but they look great and will last forever. Man-made composite countertops, such as Corian and Avonite, also are extremely durable and come in a wide choice of colors and patterns. In most cases, granite or composite tops need to be installed by professionals.

■ If you have tiling experience, you can build a countertop of ceramic or granite tile. Begin with a solid, level plywood or concrete board base. Set ceramic tiles in tile adhesive or thin-set mortar. Set granite tiles in silicone caulk. Your tile dealer can supply you with cutters for both types of materials.

1. Cut the top.
To make a sink cutout, mark the top according to manufacturer's directions; usually the hole should be 1 inch smaller than the outside dimensions of the sink. Use a sabersaw with a fine-tooth blade. To cut a ready-made top to length, turn it upside down and use a circular saw with a straightedge guide. Support the scrap carefully or the laminate will crack.

Place tape on bottom of the saw base to avoid scratching the top.

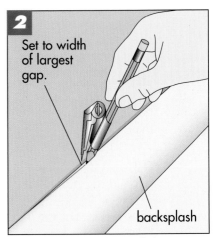
Set to width of largest gap.

backsplash

2. Scribe and belt-sand the backsplash.
Most tops have a ⅜-inch lip at the top of the backsplash that is cut easily to accommodate walls that are wavy or out of square. Set the top into place against the wall and make a scribe mark by running a compass along the wall. Don't try to cut off excess material; it will crack. Instead, use a belt sander to carefully remove the material.

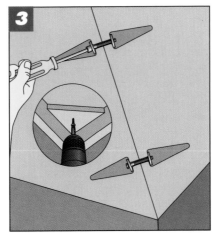

3. Assemble a splice, attach top.
Butt the pieces together on top of the base cabinets. Working from underneath, tighten the supplied bolts. Check the top as you work to make sure the splice is flat and the ends are even. To fasten the top in place (inset), drive in screws up through the cabinet framing. Screws should be long enough to hold the top, but not so long as to pierce the surface.

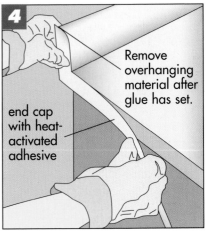
Remove overhanging material after glue has set.

end cap with heat-activated adhesive

4. Attach end caps.
For each exposed edge, buy an end cap (either left-hand or right-hand). To attach the end cap, warm it in the oven or use a household iron to melt the glue as you press it into place. Position the cap so all countertop edges are covered. Once the cap is cool, use a router or a sanding block to remove the excess material and form a uniform edge.

ORGANIZING A BEDROOM CLOSET

A typical closet with a single hanging pole and one or two long shelves makes poor use of space and is difficult to use. To upgrade your closet, custom-design it so your clothing fits without wasted space and you easily are be able to get at the things you frequently need.

You can buy ready-made storage or shelf units that are easy to install, build your own shelves and dividers out of lumber, or use a combination of the two. Keep in mind that painting wood shelves often is more time-consuming than building them.

YOU'LL NEED

TIME: For a typical 6-foot closet, a day to build an organizer.
SKILLS: Measuring and cutting, fastening with screws or nails.
TOOLS: Circular saw, tape measure, hammer, nail set, drill and screwdriver bit.

AVAILABLE ACCESSORIES

A wide variety of accessories is available to you as you make your plans for a more space-efficient and hardworking closet. Here are a few:

■ Wire-rack shelves are easy to clean and allow you to see the contents from below. Some have built-in hanging rods.
■ Drawer units are helpful for small items, especially if you do not have a dresser. Choose wire or clear-plastic drawers if you want to see your things.
■ Slide-out hampers keep your dirty clothes out of sight and make wash day easier.
■ Shoe racks make it much easier to reach your shoes and keep the closet floor clean.

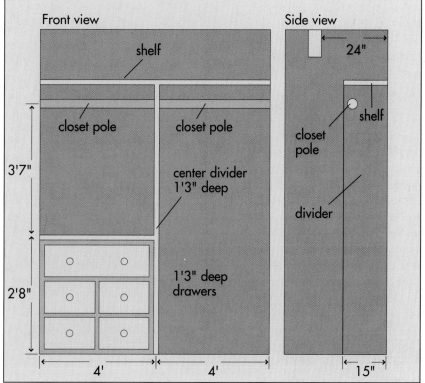

Plan a well-organized closet.
Begin by measuring and cataloging your clothes and storage items (see the chart below for some standard dimensions). By grouping clothes according to height, you can gain quite a bit of usable space. Measure the horizontal space needed for each type of clothing. Make a drawing like this one, taking into account the ¾-inch thickness of boards.

Sometimes it makes sense to begin with a set of store-bought drawers or another unit and build simple shelves around it. Be sure the closet pole is well supported every 4 feet or it will sag in time.

Decide which storage items can be placed up high and which ones you need to get at often. Avoid tall stacks of clothes and use storage boxes or wire bins where possible.

MEASUREMENTS
CLOTHING DIMENSIONS

Women's Items		Men's Items		Accessories	
Long dresses	69"	Topcoats	50"	Garment bags	57"
Robes	52"	Trousers		Hanging	
Coats	52"	(cuff-hung)	44"	shoe bags	36"
Dresses	45"	Travel bags	41"	Umbrellas and	
Skirts	35"	Suits	38"	canes	36"
Suits	29"	Shirts	28"		
Blouses	28"	Ties	27"		
		Trousers			
		(double-hung)	20"		

BUILDING SHELVES

A simple-looking shelf unit can be a surprisingly complex project. For example, middle shelves usually are slightly shorter than the bottom and top pieces. If joints are off as little as ¹⁄₁₆ inch, the whole unit may look shoddy. Even getting perfectly straight cuts can be difficult, especially if the boards are warped or bowed. But when the end result is a unit custom-made for your space, it's worth the effort. Here's how to build the dadoed shelf unit shown on *page 83*.

YOU'LL NEED

TIME: 2 hours to make the project shown on this page.
SKILLS: Accurate measuring and cutting, fastening.
TOOLS: Circular saw, tablesaw, or radial-arm saw; speed square; pencil; hammer; chisel; strap clamp.

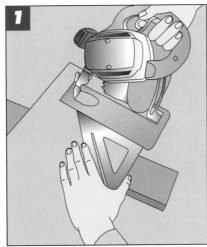

1. Cut the outside pieces.
For each outside piece, cut a miter on one end. Be sure the saw is set accurately to a 45-degree bevel; test with scrap pieces to be sure. Use a tablesaw or a radial-arm saw, or hold a speed square firmly against a factory edge as you cut with a circular saw. Measure from outside to outside—from the tip of one cut to the tip of the next.

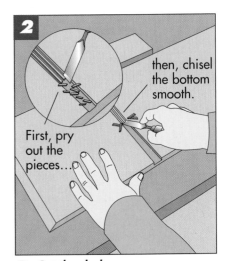

2. Cut the dadoes.
Set the two vertical outside pieces side by side and mark them for the dadoes. Set the depth of your saw blade so it cuts one-third of the way through the board. Make a series of cuts (see page 64). Clean the dadoes out by prying remaining wood out with a chisel, then smoothing the bottom with the chisel held bevel side down.

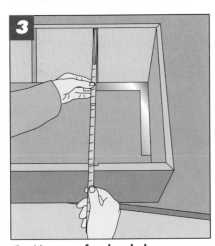

3. Measure for the shelves.
Temporarily fasten the box together by drilling pilot holes and partially driving (tacking) finishing nails at each corner. Or, use a strap clamp (see page 59). Check the box for square. Measure from the inside of each dado to inside of the corresponding dado to determine the length of each shelf. Cut the shelves to length.

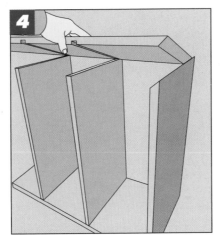

4. Assemble the pieces.
Disassemble the box. Apply glue and drive in the nails that hold one side piece to the top and bottom pieces. Carefully position these fastened pieces so the side piece is lying on a flat surface. Dry-fit the shelves into the dadoes and set the remaining side piece in place. Disassemble and make any needed adjustments. Apply glue, check for square, and nail.

5. Add the back.
Cut a piece of ¼-inch plywood or ⅛-inch hardboard for the back. It should be ¼ inch smaller than outside dimensions of the unit, so the backing edge is set back ⅛ inch. Use the back as a check to see that the unit is square. Leaving a ⅛-inch gap on all edges, fasten with 4-penny box nails every 4 inches. Fasten back to inner shelves as well as the perimeter.

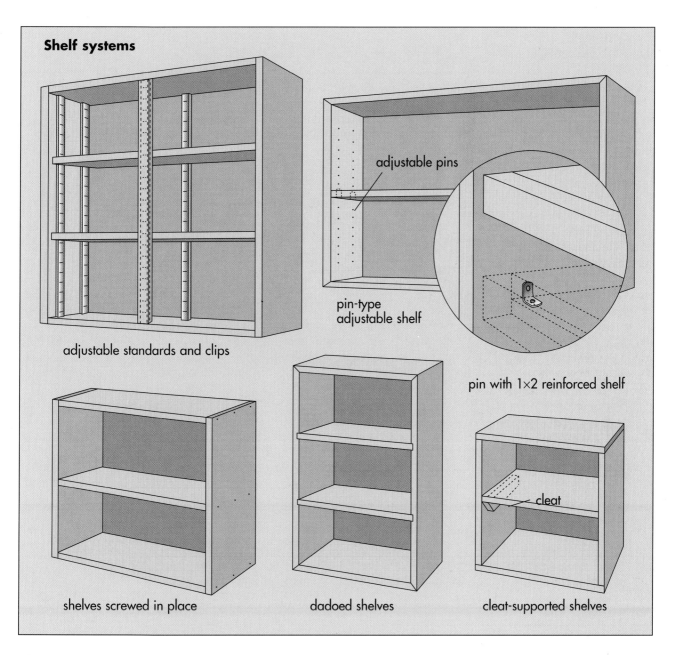

Shelf systems

adjustable standards and clips

adjustable pins

pin-type
adjustable shelf

pin with 1×2 reinforced shelf

shelves screwed in place

dadoed shelves

cleat

cleat-supported shelves

Choose between adjustable and fixed shelving.

When building a shelf system using **adjustable standards and clips** and a central vertical support, the adjustable shelves must be a smaller width than the outside pieces. For a cleaner look, set the metal standards in grooves.

To make **pin-type adjustable shelves,** precisely lay out the locations of the holes on the side pieces by clamping the sides together before marking. Use a sharp bit (hollow-point bits work well) that will not chip the surface of the wood as you bore the holes.

If a pin-type adjustable shelf unit is taller than 4 to 5 feet, it should have one or more fixed shelves to keep the side pieces from bowing out. You can add an angle bracket or wooden cleat to which you can attach the fixed shelf.

The simplest unit has **shelves screwed in place** without dadoes. Such a unit is quite strong, as long as you use three or more screws at each joint and the screws are fastened firmly. Also, use pilot holes so the wood doesn't split. Countersink the screw heads, and fill the holes with putty or plugs (see pages 46–47). If you use trim

head screws, the holes will not be much larger than those for finishing nails. To make such shelves even stronger, add cleats.

Dadoed shelves are stronger and present a clean, finished look because there is no hardware to hide. (See page 82 for how to build this unit.)

A **cleat-supported shelf** is simple to build and ideal for utility areas. Use 1×2s for the cleats. Cut the front edge of the cleat at a 45-degree angle so it's not as noticeable. Secure the cleat with countersunk screws.

HANGING SHELVES AND CABINETS ON WALLS

Any shelf system, be it simple boards or a cabinet with doors, must be hung on a wall properly. If it is not anchored into wall studs, it probably will come loose when weight is put on it. If it is not plumb and level, it will look shoddy and may even prove unsafe. As you plan your shelving, decide the following:

■ Will the shelves be supported at their ends (by the side of the shelf unit or cabinet) or from the back?

■ Do you want the shelves to be adjustable or fixed? Shelves in living areas require the versatility of adjustable hardware; utility shelves used for storage in closets, garages, and basements are fine with fixed supports.

■ Select the hardware that suits your purposes best. The chart at *bottom right* shows the most common options.

■ To make sure the shelves won't sag over time, use the span chart (below left) to determine the correct distance between shelf supports. The spacings listed there assume shelves fully loaded with books—most likely the heaviest load they'll have to bear.

■ If you opt for fixed shelves, measure the tallest items slated to go on the shelves and add at least 1 inch for overhead clearance.

SHELVING SPANS
(Assumes shelves fully loaded with books.)

Material Used	Maximum Span	Material Used	Maximum Span
¾-inch plywood	32"	2×6, 2×8 lumber	36"
¾-inch particleboard	24"	2×10, 2×12 lumber	48"
1×6, 1×8 lumber	18"	½-inch acrylic	18"
1×10, 1×12 lumber	24"	⅜-inch glass	16"

YOU'LL NEED

TIME: About 2 hours to hang an average shelf or cabinet system.
SKILLS: Measuring, plumbing, leveling, driving screws, finding wall studs.
TOOLS: Tape measure, drill, screwdriver, level.

EXPERTS' INSIGHT

PLANNING YOUR SHELF LAYOUTS

■ It may seem time-consuming, but you'll thank yourself for drawing a detailed plan of your shelf or cabinet system. Without a plan, it's hard to buy materials and easy to overlook hard-to-correct design flaws.

■ Make sure unsupported shelf ends extend no more than one-third the distance between the shelf standards.

■ If you settle on fixed shelves, maximize space by tailoring the vertical spacings so your possessions fit exactly. Keep in mind that your shelving needs may change over time. Adjustable shelves offer the best flexibility.

SHELF HARDWARE OPTIONS

Item	Application
	Rigid pressed-steel angle brackets hold medium-weight loads. For heavier loads, choose types reinforced with triangular gussets. Mount with the longer leg against the wall. Check that upper screws are fastened firmly.
	Brackets clip into slotted standards. Best way to achieve adjustable support when you can mount only from the rear. Choose 8-, 10-, or 12-inch brackets.
	For adjustable shelves with a finished appearance, mount shelves on the ends by popping pin-type clips into predrilled holes. The clips are relatively inexpensive, but the holes must be drilled precisely.
	These end-mounted adjustable standards and clips are strong but ugly. For a dressier look, rabbet the standards into the cabinet sides.
	Light-duty wire brackets are among the many accessories you can mount on perforated hardboard. Measure the thickness of the pegboard before you buy it; ¼- and ⅛-inch perforated hardboard require different bracket types.

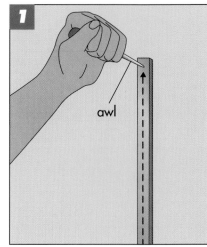

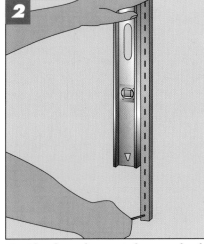

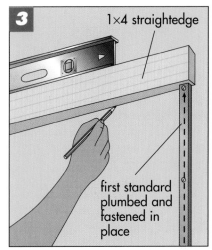

1. Mark location of standards.
Try to find at least two wall studs to support the shelf standards. To find a stud, tap the wall until you hear a dull, not a hollow, sound. Or, use a magnetic stud finder. Hammer in a small finishing nail to confirm you've found the stud. Hold one standard at the desired location and height. Mark for the top hole with an awl, then drill a pilot hole.

2. Plumb and secure the standard.
Drive in and partially tighten the screw at the top of the standard. If there is no stud, use plastic anchors or toggle bolts (see page 55). Using a carpenter's level, plumb the dangling standard, then use an awl to mark for the bottom hole. Attach it, check again that the standard is plumb, and finish securing the standard.

3. Mark for the other standards.
Run a straightedge and level from the top of the standard to the approximate location of the last standard. Strike an erasable line and step back to see if the line visually looks level. If it doesn't, redraw the line so it's parallel to the floor or an adjacent wall. Install the other standards, making sure their top ends are up.

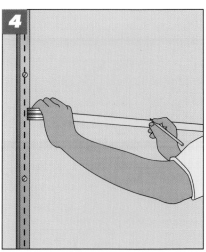

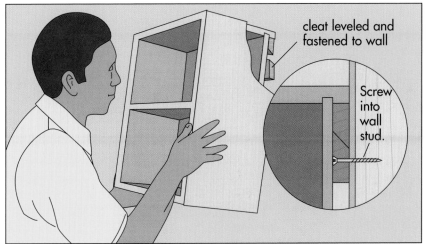

4. Install intermediate standards.
If your shelves need intermediate support, measure the distance between the end standards and divide by the number of spaces between the standards (the total number of standards minus 1). This will give you the proper spacing. However, you may want to adjust their locations so they can be attached to studs.

Mount a cabinet or shelf unit.
Of the many ways to hang cabinets on walls, the one shown above is one of the best. It provides plenty of holding power without visible screw heads or supports. It's also easy to level; you need only level the back cleat. The back of the unit, however, must be recessed ¾ inch.

Cut a 1×4 to fit behind the cabinet. Make a beveled rip cut along its center line (see pages 38 and 49–50). Attach one of the pieces to the cabinet. Level and secure the other one to the wall. Lift the unit and hold it against the wall, then slide it down onto the piece attached to the wall.

If a cabinet is well-constructed, another approach is to attach it to the wall simply by holding it in place and driving in screws through the cabinet back and into wall studs. Place screws where they will not be highly visible.

SOLVING DOOR PROBLEMS

If a door sticks or does not close properly, don't assume that you need to remove it and plane it. Analyze the situation while the door is in place. Often, screws holding the top hinge come loose, causing the door to lean. Remount the screws (see *far right*).

Loose screws, however, may be a symptom of other problems. Close the door, watching the hinge half that is connected to the jamb. If the hinge half moves, it is under stress and will come loose again. Check where the door is rubbing, scribe a line along it, and plane it.

YOU'LL NEED

TIME: 1 to 2 hours to diagnose and repair a door.
SKILLS: Close observation, planing, fastening screws.
TOOLS: Screwdriver, hammer, plane, chisel.

EXPERTS' INSIGHT

WHERE'S THE RUB?

■ When a door sticks, it is not always obvious just where the door is rubbing against the jamb. Close the door and insert a piece of cardboard into the gap between the door and the jamb. Slide it until you find a tight spot; that's where the door is sticking. For an exterior door, test the threshold as well.

■ Before making a scribe mark to plane a sticking door (see page 34), close the door to the point where it begins to stick, and no further. If the door is significantly too wide, remove the door and plane it until the door closes without straining. Then, complete the planing.

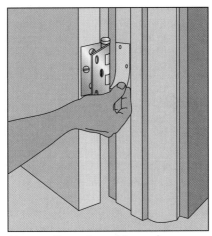

Use cardboard to shim a door.
If your door is rubbing against the jamb on the hinge side, you can relieve the pressure by shimming the hinges out. Unscrew the part of the hinge connected to the jamb and insert a piece of cardboard behind it. If a door binds at the top of the strike jamb, you may be able to fix it by shimming out the bottom hinge.

Remount and tighten hinge screws.
If hinge screws are loose, wedge the door open and remove the screws. Fold back the hinge, taking care not to lose shims that may be behind it. Whittle hole-size pieces of wood, add white glue, and push them into the holes. Chisel the plugs flush, fold the hinge back, drill pilot holes, and redrive the screws.

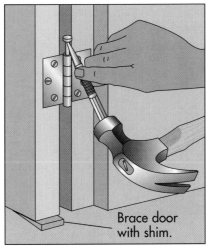

Brace door with shim.

Remove a door.
If the door needs to be modified so it will fit, mark it with clear scribe lines. You probably will need to remove it to get at the edges that need planing. Tap the hinge pins out with a nail set, removing the bottom pin first. If the hinges are old and the pins are solidly rusted or painted in place, you'll have to unscrew the hinges from the door to remove it.

Plane the door.
Set the door on its edge on a flat surface. Brace it in a corner so it will not move as you work. If you need to plane the whole edge, work inward from each end toward the middle to avoid splintering (see pages 66–67). If you have to remove a lot of material, rip-saw the door with a circular saw, then plane it smooth.

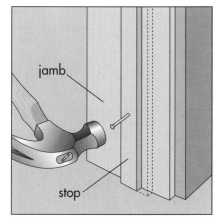

Move the stop to correct a bind.
Sometimes a door will bind against the stop on the hinge side, or it will not close properly because the stop on the latch side is placed improperly. In either case, it is much easier to move the stop than to unwarp a door. Pry the stop off. Close the door and scribe a line on the jamb along the door's inside edge. Renail the stop on this line.

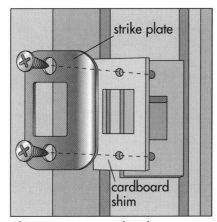

Shim or move a strike plate.
If a strike plate is too far away for the door latch to engage it, shim it out with cardboard shims. Often a latch and strike will get out of alignment because the house has settled. If this occurs, unscrew the strike, chisel out a new mortise where necessary, drill pilot holes, and reinstall the strike. Fill the old mortise cavity with wood putty and sand it smooth.

CUTTING A DOOR

When cutting off a panel door, use a knife to cut a line wherever you will be cutting across the grain. To avoid splintering the door face, make your saw cut below that line.

Newer, solid-core doors are filled with a soft type of particleboard; there is solid wood only for an inch or so around the door perimeter. If you have to cut off more than an inch on such a door, the particleboard will be exposed and will require a couple of coats of sealer.

Trimming a hollow-core door is more complex (see steps, *right*).

YOU'LL NEED
TIME: About 2 hours to cut down a hollow-core door.
SKILLS: Measuring, cutting a straight line, smoothing.
TOOLS: Knife, circular saw, straightedge, chisel, hammer.

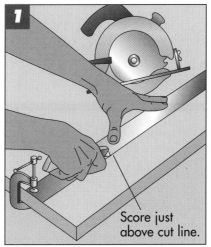

Score just above cut line.

1. Cut the veneer, then the door.
With a straightedge clamped in position, use a sharp utility knife to cut through the veneer about $1/16$ inch above where you want your final cut. It may take several passes with your knife to do this. Move and clamp the straightedge into final position and complete the cut with a circular saw (see page 38).

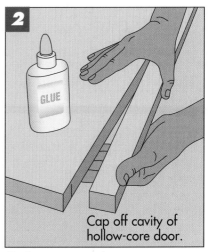

Cap off cavity of hollow-core door.

2. Insert a cap piece.
If you cut off more than about an inch of a hollow-core door, the door will be hollow at the place you just cut. Clear out some of the cardboard webbing with a chisel. Rip a piece of softwood to the required width and length. Apply white glue to both sides of the piece and tap it into position. Clamp firmly until the glue is set.

INSTALLING DOOR HINGES AND LOCKSETS

A door that swings easily on neatly installed hinges is the hallmark of a good carpenter. Hanging a door is not an easy job, but if you have patience, take things step by step, and pay attention to details, you can learn how to install a door that swings freely and shuts firmly.

If you are replacing an old door that was damaged, chances are good that the door opening is not square. Cutting the door to fit will be the first and most difficult task. If the old door fit well, use it as a template. Simply remove the old hardware, lay it on top of your new door, and trace for trimming. If the old door did not fit well, have a helper hold the new door in place while you shim it into final position. Carefully scribe the cut lines. If the door jamb is damaged and must be replaced, try to square the opening when you install the new jamb. Or, install a prehung door (page 90).

There is a strict order to hanging doors. First hang the door and make sure it swings freely and closes tightly against the door stop. Next install the lockset. Finally cut the hole for and install the strike plate.

YOU'LL NEED

TIME: About 3 hours to hang a door and install a new lockset and deadbolt.
SKILLS: Measuring precisely, chiseling, drilling, and fastening with screws.
TOOLS: Drill with the correct bits (check the lockset instructions), utility knife or butt marker, tape measure, center punch, screwdriver, hammer, chisel.

1. Mark for the hinge locations.
Leave half of the hinge on the door jamb. Set the door in place, using shims to wedge it exactly in place. Make sure the gaps at the bottom and the top of the door are even. With a pencil or a knife, carefully mark for the location of the hinges by marking the bottom and top of each hinge.

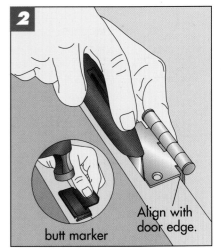

Align with door edge.

butt marker

2. Scribe marks for the hinges.
Mark the outline of the hinges by holding the hinge in place as a template. Use a utility knife to make a light mark around the hinge. A handy tool called a butt marker (see inset, *above*) has chisel edges that will make indentations for a perfect cut. Hold it in place and pound on it with a hammer.

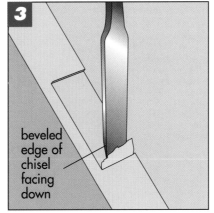

beveled edge of chisel facing down

3. Chisel the mortise.
With a knife or a chisel, deepen the lines marking the outside edges of the hinge until they are the full depth of the mortise. Holding the chisel with the beveled edge down, cut away enough material so that the hinge half sits flush with the surface of the door edge.

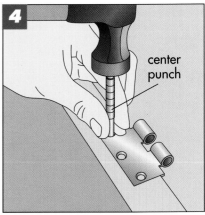

center punch

4. Install the hinge.
Remove the pin from the hinge and install the separate halves on the door and jamb. Position a hinge half in its mortise and mark it for drilling with a center punch. Be careful to drill straight pilot holes or the screw heads won't sit flush. Drive screws into all the holes. Hang the door by aligning the hinge sections and reinserting the pin.

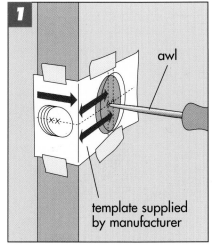

1. Mark holes for a lockset or deadbolt.

Locksets or deadbolts come with paper or cardboard templates to help position them on the door. If a strike plate exists in the jamb, align the template with it so you won't have to cut a new mortise in it. Tape or hold it against the door, as shown. With an awl or the point of a spade bit, mark for the holes in the door face and edge by piercing through the template.

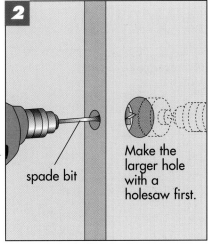

2. Drill the holes.

Drill the hole through the face of the door first, using a holesaw. To avoid splintering the veneer, drill just far enough so the pilot bit of the holesaw pokes through the other side. Then drill from the other side. Use a spade bit to drill through the edge; be sure to hold the bit parallel to the surface of the door and perpendicular to its edge. Some locksets require that you continue drilling into the rear of the large hole another half inch.

TOOLS TO USE

SELECT THE CORRECT DRILL BITS

■ Most lockset manufacturers call for a 2⅛-inch hole in the face of the door and a ⅞-inch hole in the door edge. But don't take that for granted; some call for other sizes. When you buy the handle or lockset, check the instructions and buy the right drill bits at the same time.

■ A standard holesaw works best for the large hole, but if you aren't going to install locksets very often, you may want to get an adjustable hole cutter. It will cut more slowly, but you can use it for different sizes of holes in other projects.

■ A spade bit works fine for the smaller hole, but if you want a more precise cut, use a hand brace and auger bit.

3. Mortise the latch bolt.

Insert the bolt through the smaller hole and hold it centered in the door while you mark for its mortise. Use a sharp pencil or a knife to mark the outline. Cut and chisel a mortise as you did for the hinges (see page 88). Depending on the type of bolt, this mortise may need to be deeper near the center than at the edges.

4. Install bolt and/or handles.

Install the bolt by setting it in the mortise, drilling pilot holes, and driving in the screws provided. Install the lockset or handles according to the manufacturer's directions. Tighten all screws. Test the mechanisms to make sure they operate smoothly; you may need to clean out or widen your holes.

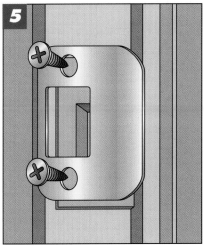

5. Install the strike plate.

Mark the jamb for the correct location of the strike plate. The latch or bolt should be centered vertically in the strike opening. Make sure the latch or bolt enters the door jamb while holding it fairly tight against the door stop. Mortise the jamb, drill pilot holes, and install the strike with the screws provided.

INSTALLING PREHUNG DOORS

A prehung door costs a little more than buying a door, jamb, and the trim separately. But it will save you loads of time and probably will result in a better installation. With a prehung door, you'll avoid having to cut the jamb, three stop pieces, and six casing pieces; mortise and install hinges; and drill and mortise for the handle and the strike plate.

Before you order a prehung unit, measure not only the width and height of your opening, but also the thickness of the wall.

YOU'LL NEED

TIME: 2 hours to install a prehung unit in a rough opening.
SKILLS: Nailing, leveling, and shimming.
TOOLS: Hammer, level, framing square, shims.

Install a standard prehung door.
Set the door into the opening and shim it if necessary to plumb it. Temporarily attach the hinge side of the jamb to the framing. Check the other two jamb pieces for square with a framing square and by closing the door; the gap should be even all around. Shim and attach all sides of the jamb. Install the casing.

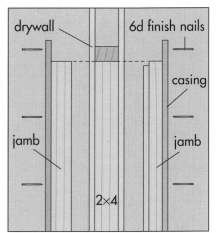

Install a split-style prehung door.
With this type of prehung door, the jamb is split, and the casing remains attached to the two jamb halves. Install the jamb half that has the door attached, just as you would a standard prehung door. Slip in the second half and cover the joint between the two with the stop molding provided.

INSTALLING A DEADBOLT LOCK

Deadbolt locks are a fairly easy way to add security to a door. These locks have long bolts that reach into the jamb and sometimes through to the framing.

A double-keyed deadbolt, which locks with a key on the inside as well as the outside, offers the best security in situations where an intruder could reach through a window to the bolt. However, it is not safe in cases of fire—if you don't have the key handy, you could be stuck inside.

YOU'LL NEED

TIME: About 1 hour.
SKILLS: Drilling holes, mortising, assembling parts.
TOOLS: Drill with the required bits, chisel, knife.

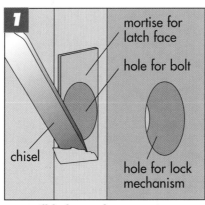

1. Drill holes and cut mortise.
Following the same techniques as for a lockset (see page 89), mark for the position of the two holes and drill them, taking care to hold the drill perpendicular. Insert the bolt and latch face into their hole and mark for the mortise with a sharp knife. Cut the mortise with a chisel (see page 88).

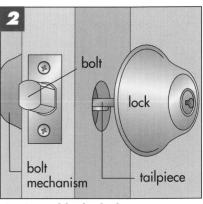

2. Assemble the lock.
Screw the latch face into the mortise. For many lock types, you'll need to use a screwdriver to partially extend the bolt. Insert the lock tailpiece through the slot in the bolt mechanism and slip on the interior turn bolt or lock until the two pieces sit flush against the door. Fasten the retaining screws. Install the strike plate.

BUILDING A WALL

Behind most finished residential walls lies a rather simple construction. Vertical members, called studs, butt at the top and bottom against horizontal members, called plates. Although it looks straightforward, building a wall takes thoughtful planning. When you cover the framing with sheets of drywall or paneling, the seams between sheets must fall in the center of studs. There must be a nailing surface for the sheets at all the corners (see page 94). And, all framing members must be aligned along a flat plane.

If the floor and ceiling are nearly level, it's rather easy to preassemble a stud wall on the floor and then raise it into position. If the floor and ceiling are uneven, or if you're building the wall in tight quarters, it's best to build the wall in place, custom-cutting each stud to fit and toenailing it to the top and bottom plates (see pages 93–94).

Whichever approach you choose, make sure you have a way to attach your wall to the ceiling. If the wall runs perpendicular to the ceiling joists, simply fasten the wall's top plate with two 16-penny nails at every joist. If it runs parallel to the joists, you will have to install cross braces, so you can nail the top plate into solid material (see page 92).

YOU'LL NEED

TIME: About 2 hours to build a simple 10-foot wall; longer if you need to build it in place or in awkward situations.
SKILLS: Cutting, measuring, fastening with nails.
TOOLS: Tape measure, chalk line, pencil, framing square, saw, speed or combination square, level, hammer.

1. Mark the wall location.
Begin by deciding exactly where the wall will go. Use a framing square and a chalk line to mark its location on the floor. For long walls, check for square using the 3-4-5 method (see page 32).

Using a level and a straight 2×4 that is as high as your ceiling, mark the wall location on the ceiling, joists, or cross bracing. These marks will help you position the wall before you plumb it. Make sure there is adequate framing in the ceiling to which you can nail the top plate.

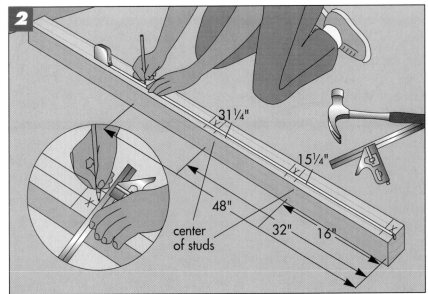

2. Cut and mark the plates.
Using your floor layout as a guide, mark and cut 2×4s for the top and bottom plates (usually the same length). Place them on edge beside each other and mark for the studs. The first stud will be at the end of the wall. The remaining studs should be 16 (or 24) inches on center, meaning that from the edge of the wall to the center of each stud will be a multiple of 16 (or 24). Make a mark every 16 inches; then with a combination or speed square draw lines ¾ inch on each side of your first marks. Draw an X in the middle of the marks to show where to nail the studs.

BUILDING A WALL

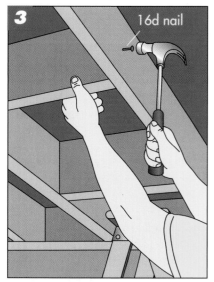

3. Provide nailers, cut studs.

If your new wall runs parallel to the ceiling joists, cut pieces of 2× material to fit tightly between the ceiling joists and install them every 2 feet or so. Measure for your studs (see page 93) and cut them to length.

4. Assemble the wall.

Working on a flat surface, lay the studs on edge between the top and bottom plates. It helps to have something solid, such as a wall, to hold the framing against while you assemble and nail the wall.

For speed, nail one plate at a time to the studs. Drive two 16- penny nails through the plate and into the ends of each stud. Because hammer blows tend to knock studs out of alignment, continually double-check your work while nailing. Keep the edges of the studs flush with the plate edges. If any of the studs are twisted or bowed, replace them.

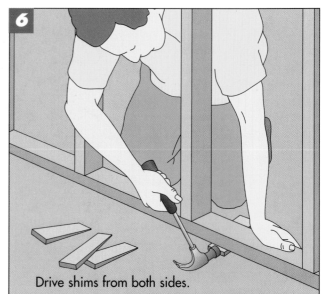

Drive shims from both sides.

5. Raise the frame.

Framework can be cumbersome, so have a helper on hand. Position the bottom plate about where it needs to go and tip the wall into position. If the wall fits so tightly against the ceiling that you have to hammer it into place, protect the framing with a scrap of 2×4 as you pound. Tap both ends of the frame until it is roughly plumb in both directions.

6. Snug the frame with shims.

If the wall is a bit short in places, drive shims between the bottom plate and the floor or between the top plate and the ceiling joists. Have your helper steady the framework while you drive the pieces in place. Drive shims in from both sides, thin edge to thin edge, to keep the plate from tilting.

7. Fasten frame to wall and floor.
Once the frame is snug, recheck that the wall is plumb in both directions. Check both ends of the wall and every other stud. Fasten the top plate to the ceiling by driving in a 16-penny nail through the plate and into each joist. Fasten the bottom plate to the floor. Use 16-penny nails if the floor is wood; use masonry nails or a power hammer if the floor is concrete (see page 99).

MEASUREMENTS

GETTING THE STUD LENGTH CORRECT

Few things are more frustrating than building a stud wall only to find that your measurements were off and the wall is ¼ inch too tall. When that happens, the only thing you can do is take the wall down, pull off one plate, remove the nails, cut all the studs, and nail it back together again.

To measure for stud length, nail together two scraps of 2×4 to represent the top and bottom plates. Set this double 2×4 on the floor, measure up to the joist, and subtract ¼ inch for shimming. Take measurements every few feet.

BUILDING A WALL IN PLACE

1. Install top and bottom plates.
If building a wall on the floor and raising it into position are not practical in your situation, begin by cutting the top and bottom plates, and marking them for studs (see page 91). Transfer the marks to the faces of the plates, making sure the marks are clear so you can see them easily to align the studs while toenailing.

Nail the top plate to the joists. Use a level and a straight board to mark the location of the bottom plate or use a chalk line case as a plumb bob. Mark the floor in two places and make an X to indicate on which side of the mark the plate should be positioned. Use masonry nails or a power hammer to fasten the bottom plate to the floor (see page 99).

16d nails

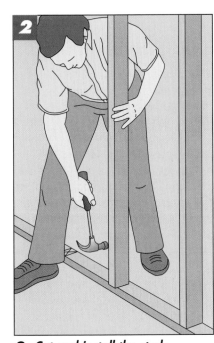

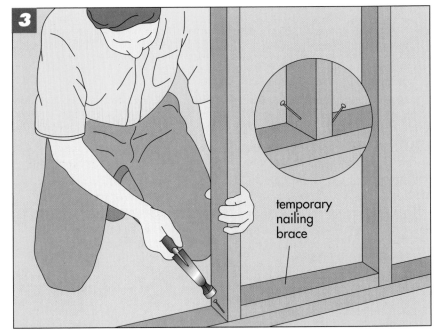

2. Cut and install the studs.

With top and bottom plates installed, measure the required length of each stud individually. Add ¹⁄₁₆ inch for a snug fit and cut. Tap each stud into place. If you really have to whack it to get it into place, it is too long. Don't risk splitting the stud; take it down and trim it a little.

3. Toenail the studs.

To secure the studs, drive 8-penny nails at an angle through the side of studs and into the plate; this is called toenailing. Tap the nail once or twice while holding it parallel to the floor or ceiling. When the nail tip bites into the wood, change the angle to 45 degrees. Drive four to six nails into each joint, two on each side, with an optional one at the front and back. The first nail may move the stud, but the second nail, driven from the other side, will move it back.

If you have difficulty toenailing, drill pilot holes for the nails, using a ³⁄₃₂-inch bit. Or, place a 14¹⁄₂-inch board between studs to serve as a temporary nailing brace.

4. Frame at corners.

When framing corners, make sure there is a nailing surface for every piece of drywall or paneling that will be installed. This means adding nonstructural nailers.

In Situation 1, *right,* the extra stud is turned sideways to offer a nailing surface and strengthen the corner. Drive 16-penny nails first through end stud #1 and into the extra stud, then through end stud #2 and into the extra stud and end stud #1.

In Situation 2, *right,* several foot-long 2×4 scraps (usually three in a standard 8-foot wall) serve as spacers between two full-length studs placed at the end of one wall. Tie the wall sections together with 16-penny nails.

Situation 3, *right,* shows two intersecting walls. Nail three studs together and to the plates, then attach to the adjoining wall.

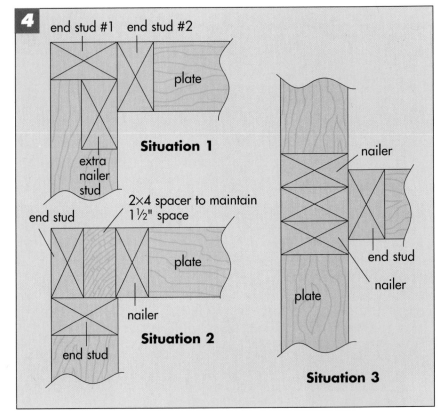

ROUGHING-IN AN OPENING

If you plan to install a door in your wall, find out the rough opening dimensions you'll need. For a prehung door, measure the outside dimensions of the jamb and add ½ inch for shimming. With a slab door (one that is not prehung), measure the width of the door, add 2½ inches for the side jambs and shims, and add 2 inches to the height for the head jamb, shims, and flooring. Standard door widths are 24, 26, 28, 30, 32, and 36 inches. Door heights usually are 80 inches.

Once you know the opening's size, build the wall as described on pages 91–94, with the addition of the framing members shown below. These framing members have special names and functions.

Jack studs are the vertical 2×4s on each side of the door opening. They are attached to a **king stud** or to another jack stud. This doubling of studs provides solid, unbending support for the door.

The **header** is made of two 2×6s with a ½-inch plywood spacer sandwiched in between. (The plywood is needed to make the header 3½ inches thick, the same thickness as the wall framing.) The header rests on top of the jack studs and spans the top of the opening, supporting overhead loads. For openings that are less than 3 feet wide, you can use 2×4s instead of 2×6s.

Cripples are the short 2×4s added between the header and the top plate. They maintain a 16-inch on-center stud spacing for nailing the drywall and help distribute the weight equally from above.

A window opening is much like a door opening. You install a sill (much like a header) at the bottom height of the window and add more cripples between it and the wall's bottom plate.

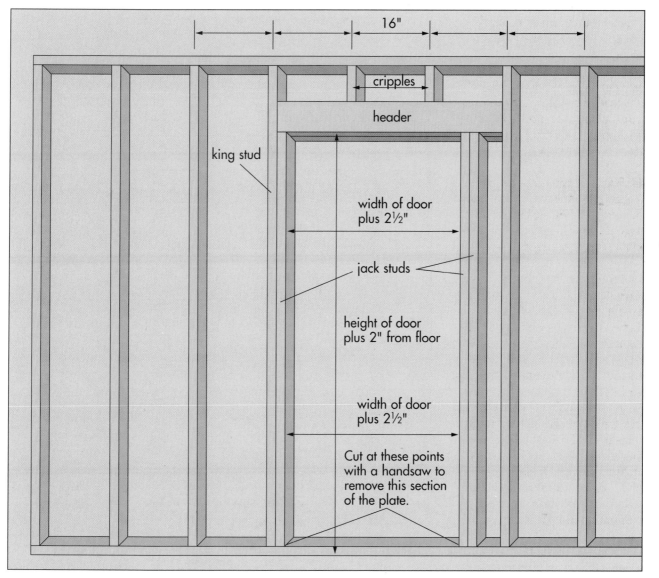

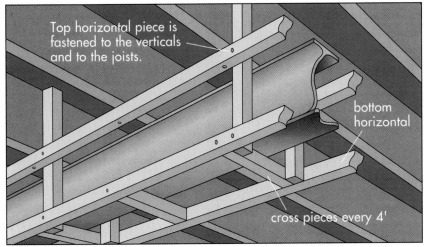

Frame around an I-beam.

Use 2×2s to frame around a narrow obstruction, such as a beam. Fasten the frame together with screws rather than nails because the structure will be wobbly as you work. Drill pilot holes whenever you drive a screw near the end of a board.

Make chalk lines on the joists, 1⅝ inches out from either side of the beam. On every other joist, attach a vertical 2×2 to the joists, cutting them to extend 1¾ inches below the bottom of the beam. Fasten horizontal pieces to the bottom ends of the verticals, then fasten horizontal pieces at the top, driving screws into both the vertical supports and the joists. Finish the framing by installing short horizontal cross pieces about every 4 feet between the bottom horizontal frame members.

Frame around a pipe.

You can cover a soil stack or other tall, narrow obstruction with a frame. Mark lines on the floor and measure for top and bottom plates as you would a regular wall. Draw plumb lines on the walls to use as guides. Build three narrow walls of 2×4s or 2×2s; raise them into position; and fasten them to the floor, ceiling, wall, and each other.

WORKING WITH METAL STUDS

Metal framing costs a good deal less than wood 2×4s, and it is lighter. Metal is not susceptible to rot or insect damage, and the factory-made pieces are free from bows, twists, knots, and other imperfections that sometimes make wood hard to work with.

Working with metal studs takes some adjustments. You can't build walls on the floor then raise them up. Instead, you must install the top and floor runners, then insert the studs. Cut metal studs with tin snips or a circular saw and metal-cutting blade. Fasten the pieces together with self-tapping screws.

If you make a mistake, it usually is easier to move a metal stud than a wood one. Running electrical wiring and pipes for plumbing is easy because punchout holes are precut in the studs.

On the downside, once walls are built, you can't attach items to metal stud walls as easily as you can with wood walls. You can fasten items to a metal stud with a screw, but not a nail. If you plan to hang cabinets or shelves on the wall, cross-brace the wall with C-runners. Door jambs and windows can be attached to steel framing, but it's easier to shim and attach the units if you use wood framing, fastened to the metal studs, around these openings.

YOU'LL NEED

TIME: 1 to 2 hours to build a basic 12-foot wall.

SKILLS: Measuring and marking for walls, cutting with tin snips, fastening with a drill or screw gun.

TOOLS: Tape measure, level, tin snips or circular saw with metal-cutting blade, drill or screw gun, plumb bob.

CAUTION!
WATCH OUT FOR METAL

■ *The ends of metal studs, especially those that you cut, often are very sharp. When working with metal, wear gloves. If you're cutting with a circular saw and metal cutting blade, wear long sleeves that are not loose or floppy.*

■ *Cutting metal also can be dangerous because small pieces of metal fly through the air. Be sure to wear eye protection whenever you cut metal studs.*

■ *If you run electrical wiring through metal framing, use sections of plastic foam pipe insulation (see page 97) or specially made plastic grommets to protect wires from damage.*

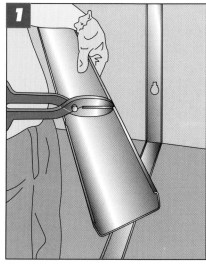

1. Cut the studs.

Lay out the framing as you would for a wood wall (see pages 92–94). Cut the runners to be used for top and bottom plates to length with tin snips. Or, use a metal-cutting blade on a circular saw. Using a circular saw is faster, but make sure no one is in the area as you cut and wear protective eye wear and clothing as you work.

2. Attach the ceiling runner.

Position the ceiling runner and attach it to each joist with a drywall screw. If joists run parallel to the wall, install cross-bracing so there is something to which you can attach the runner. Position the floor runner directly below the ceiling runner, using a plumb bob. Attach it to the floor with screws or masonry nails.

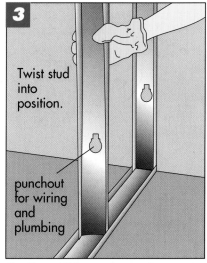

3. Cut and insert the studs.

Cut the studs to length with tin snips. Insert them into the runners, starting at a slight angle and twisting them into place. For easier plumbing or electrical installation, make sure all the stud legs are pointed in the same direction and all the predrilled punchouts line up.

4. Attach studs to the runners.

Once studs are placed correctly, drive in $7/16$-inch pan- or wafer-headed screws through the runners and into the studs. Hold the stud flange firmly against the runner as you work. Drive in four screws, one on either side of each runner at the top and bottom.

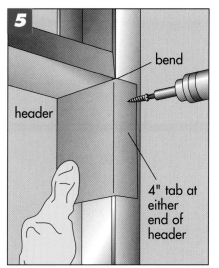

5. Attach headers.

Where you need a door or window header, cut a stud piece 8 inches longer than the width of the opening. Cut the two sides of the stud 4 inches from each end so you can bend back a tab, as shown. Slip the tabs into place and attach with screws.

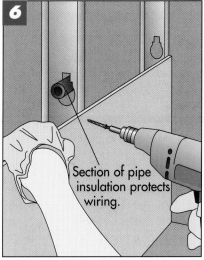

6. Install the drywall.

Inspect the framing to make sure you have a fastening surface for drywall at all points. Attach the drywall with drywall screws placed 8 to 12 inches apart. Install corner beads with screws or staples. Tape and finish the walls (see pages 100–103).

FURRING BASEMENT WALLS

When finishing basement walls, one option is to build regular stud walls (see pages 91–97), and fasten them to the concrete or masonry walls. A stud wall goes up quickly, gives you room to add plenty of insulation, and ensures that the new walls will be straight, even if the existing walls are not. The disadvantage is you lose some floor space because of the thickness of the walls.

If insulation is not a problem and your basement walls are fairly smooth and straight, you may want to save money in materials and preserve some square footage by building the walls with 1×2, 1×3, or 1×4 furring strips.

The layout is the same as for stud walls. The seams between drywall or paneling sheets must fall on a furring strip, and there must be a nailing surface in all corners and at ends of the sheets.

The construction method, however, is much different. Furring strips are shimmed where necessary, then fastened with glue and masonry nails or with a power hammer, which shoots nails with gunpowder charges (see page 99).

YOU'LL NEED

TIME: 1 day for a 12×12-foot room.
SKILLS: Laying out, measuring, cutting, and hammering.
TOOLS: Hammer, baby sledge, caulking gun, circular saw, tape measure, level, chalk line.

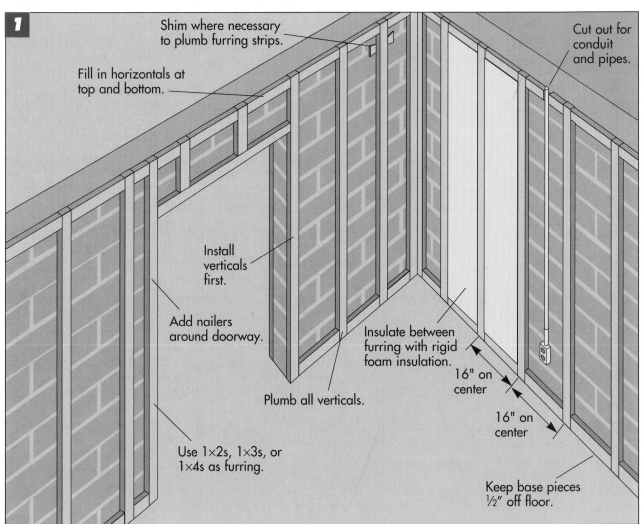

1

Shim where necessary to plumb furring strips.

Fill in horizontals at top and bottom.

Install verticals first.

Add nailers around doorway.

Plumb all verticals.

Use 1×2s, 1×3s, or 1×4s as furring.

Insulate between furring with rigid foam insulation.

Cut out for conduit and pipes.

16" on center

16" on center

Keep base pieces ½" off floor.

1. Plan the furring layout.
Begin the job by marking the locations of the vertical furring strips. One easy way to do this is to position a sheet of your wall material in the corner of the room, plumb it, and strike a chalk line down its outside edge. Using this line as a guide and 16 inches as the center-to-center measurement, mark the locations of the other vertical strips along that wall.

Measure and cut each strip to fit between the floor and ceiling. Cut each piece ½ inch short, so that it will be fastened a bit above the floor as a safeguard against flooding and settling.

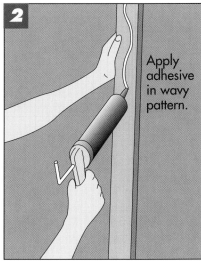

2. Apply adhesive.

With a caulking gun, squeeze a wavy ¼-inch bead of construction adhesive onto the furring strip. As you finish, turn the gun's handle to ease pressure on the adhesive, discontinuing the flow. Push the strip against the wall in its correct location, pressing firmly to help spread the adhesive.

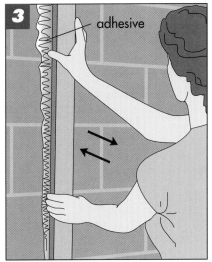

3. Set adhesive.

Pull the strip off the wall and lean it against another wall to dry and let the adhesive begin to set up. After letting it set for the time specified by the manufacturer, press the strip back into place.

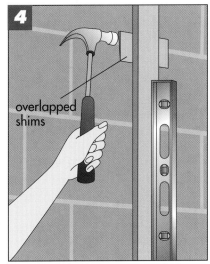

4. Plumb and shim as needed.

Check the strip for plumb. If a dip or bulge is noticeable to the eye, tuck pairs of shims behind the strip and wedge it into line. Double-check your work as the job progresses by holding a straightedge horizontally across four or five vertical pieces. Correct any gaps or bulges.

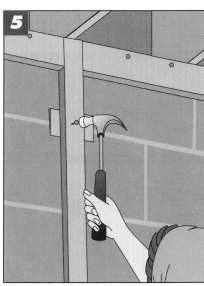

5. Drive in fasteners.

Hammer concrete nails through the strip and the shims and into the masonry wall. On a brick or block wall, it often is easiest to drive the nails into the mortar joints. Use a baby sledge if you have one. Driving nails into concrete walls is extremely difficult; consider a power hammer (see box at right).

6. Install the horizontal pieces.

After all the verticals are in place, aligned, and secured, begin work on the top and bottom horizontal pieces. Measure and cut them one at a time. Apply adhesive, shim if necessary, and install them as you did the verticals.

TOOLS TO USE

POWER HAMMER

Choose a power hammer that loads quickly. It usually makes sense to rent a better-quality power tool, rather than buying a cheap one. Experiment with several types of loads to find one powerful enough to drive in the nails completely, but not so powerful as to drive them through the furring strips. **Note:** *Follow the manufacturer's directions carefully. A power hammer is literally a firearm, and is dangerous if mishandled.*

QUART-SIZE CAULKING GUN

On large jobs, this tool will pay for itself because adhesive purchased in large tubes costs less per ounce. It also will save you time and create less mess because you'll need to change tubes 2½ times less often.

LAYING OUT AND CUTTING DRYWALL

Drywall is inexpensive, and hanging and finishing skills are within the reach of a homeowner. But hanging drywall is difficult work. The sheets are heavy and unwieldy because they are so large. Most rooms are out of square, so cutting is often difficult.

Finishing drywall to a perfectly smooth surface takes three applications of compound and sandings for professionals—four or five for beginners. Finishing success relies in part on careful hanging. So, this is one job you may want to get estimates for hanging and finishing and hire the job out to a professional.

Check framing to make sure you have adequate nailing surfaces (see page 94). Add members that are missing. If you are covering an existing wall, locate all the joists and studs and clearly mark their locations on the walls and ceilings. Draft a strong helper—hanging drywall alone is nearly impossible.

YOU'LL NEED
TIME: With a helper, a day to drywall a 12×12-foot room.
SKILLS: Measuring, physical strength, thoroughness.
TOOLS: Tape measure, drywall square, utility knife, drywall saw, chalk line.

TOOLS TO USE

DRYWALL SQUARE
Don't hesitate to spend the money for a drywall square (see page 10). It quickly pays for itself in time and labor savings. For crosscuts, you simply make one measurement, set the square in place, and run your knife along the square's blade for a square cut. It also simplifies rip cuts (see page 101).

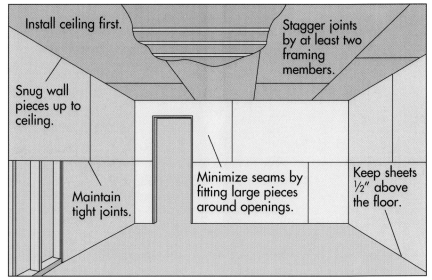

Install ceiling first.

Stagger joints by at least two framing members.

Snug wall pieces up to ceiling.

Maintain tight joints.

Minimize seams by fitting large pieces around openings.

Keep sheets ½" above the floor.

Lay out the job.
Plan where each sheet will go. Begin by hanging sheets on the ceiling, then butt the wall pieces up against the ceiling. Remember that taping and finishing (see pages 104–105) the drywall takes more time than hanging it (see pages 102–103), so minimize seams wherever possible. Sometimes you can eliminate a butt seam, which is the hardest type of seam to tape, by using 10- or 12-foot sheets instead of standard 8-foot sheets. Installing these big sheets may seem like a lot of trouble, but it will save you time and effort in the long run.

Trap with foot.

Cut backing after break.

Make a crosscut.
Store drywall sheets flat or on edge on pieces of 1× or 2× scrap lumber to hold the sheets off the floor. Before cutting a sheet, make sure the finished surface is facing you. Mark your cut line, stand the sheet on edge, and set your drywall square in place. Clasp the square firmly on top, and brace it at its base with your foot. With the edge of the knife blade against the square, cut downward most of the way, then finish by cutting up from the bottom. Snap the segment back away from your cut line. Finally slice through the backing paper with your knife.

Measure for the last piece.
To determine the correct cutoff length of a corner sheet, measure the distance from the last sheet to the corner at both the top and the bottom. If it is more than ¼ inch out of square, mark both ends of the cut, rather than making a square cut with a drywall square.

Slide the square and the knife together.

Make a rip cut.
If you need to make a parallel rip cut—one that is the same width all along its length—use your drywall square. Set the square on the edge of the sheet, and hold the knife against it at the measured distance. Slide the square along with the knife in

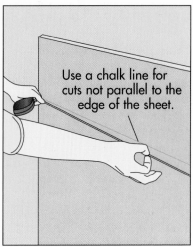

Use a chalk line for cuts not parallel to the edge of the sheet.

position, cutting as you go.

Often a rip cut will not be square; it will be shorter at one end than the other. In this case, make a mark at each end of the sheet and chalk a line between the marks. Cut freehand or use a straightedge as a guide if you need precision.

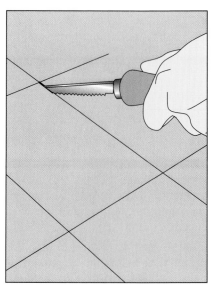

Make a rectangular cutout.
To make a cut for a receptacle box, measure the distance from the box edges to the edge of the last panel. Then measure the distance from the top and bottom of the electrical box to the floor (minus ½ inch) or from the piece above it. Transfer the measurements to the sheet and draw a rectangle. Score the surface with a utility knife, then cut it with a drywall saw.

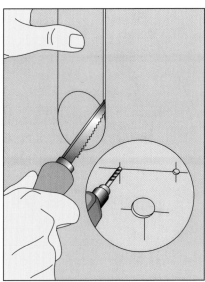

Cut around pipes.
To cut a hole for a pipe, measure and mark the sheet for the center of the pipe. Drill a hole using a holesaw bit that is slightly larger than the pipe diameter. Or, you can draw a circle and cut it out with a drywall saw or a knife.

EXPERTS' INSIGHT

AVOID MOISTURE DAMAGE IN A BASEMENT

■ Wood framing can withstand occasional wetness as long as it is allowed to dry out. But drywall that gets wet once will lose its strength and crumble.

■ If you are drywalling a basement or another place that is subject to chronic dampness or occasional flooding, add nailers to the base of the framing and cut the drywall sheets so they are held off the floor 2 to 3 inches. When you install the baseboard molding, you will need to fur out the gap.

■ To raise drywall even higher, add a 1×6 baseboard directly to the framing and set the drywall on top of it. This will keep the drywall 5½ inches off the floor.

HANGING DRYWALL

Be prepared for strenuous labor when it comes time to hang drywall. The sheets are heavy, you'll be working in awkward positions, and you'll have to hold the sheets in place while you drive in nails or screws. It's tempting to rush the job, but you'll kick yourself later if you do sloppy work. Wide gaps between drywall sheets take a long time to tape, and nobody wants nails popping out later. Here's how to do the job correctly the first time.

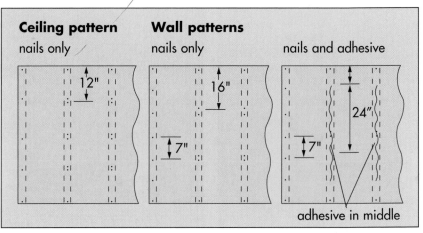

Ceiling pattern
nails only

Wall patterns
nails only

nails and adhesive

adhesive in middle

YOU'LL NEED

TIME: 20 minutes per sheet for walls, 30 minutes per ceiling sheet.
SKILLS: A strong back, fastening in difficult circumstances.
TOOLS: Tape measure, good ladders or scaffolding, hammer or drill with drywall-type screwdriver attachment, drywall taping blades.

Nail or screw according to code.

Local building codes specify how many nails or screws you should use to hang drywall and in what sort of pattern. Codes vary not only from region to region, but from room to room; for example, more fasteners may be required in bathrooms. Check with your building department.

Many professionals don't nail in pairs, but there is good reason to do so: If one nail pops through the paper, the other will hold.

For ceiling panels, the general practice is to pair nails at 12-inch intervals around the perimeter and 12 inches along each joist. Requirements are less stringent for walls. If you don't use adhesive, install two nails into the wall studs at 16-inch intervals and a single nail every 7 inches along edges. When using adhesive, install two nails at 24-inch intervals and one nail at 7 inches along the edge. Keep adhesive 6 inches away from top and bottom of sheet.

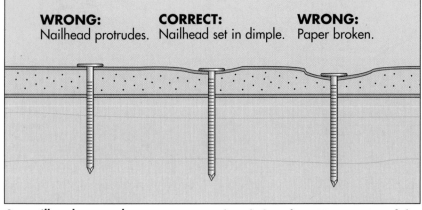

WRONG:
Nailhead protrudes.

CORRECT:
Nailhead set in dimple.

WRONG:
Paper broken.

Set nailheads correctly.

If you simply drive in a nail flush, you will not be able to cover over it with joint compound. If you drive the nail too deeply, you will break the paper on the drywall. When the paper is broken, the nail won't hold; it tears right through the gypsum inner core.

Try to drive the nail so the nailhead is set into a slightly dimpled surface. No portion of the nailhead should protrude above the surface of the drywall.

To test if your nails are driven deeply enough, run a taping blade along the surface of the wall. You should not feel any nailheads click against the blade as you pull it across. Pull out any nails that miss a joist or stud. Swat the hole with your hammer to dimple it.

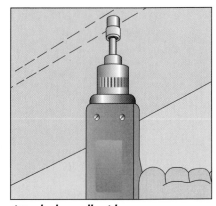

Attach drywall with screws.

If you are using screws, the same principles apply as with nailing: The screw head must be set below the surface, but it must not break the paper. This is difficult to do with a simple screwdriver bit. Use a dimpler bit or a drywall screwdriver (see box on page 103). Always drive in screws perpendicular to the sheet or their heads will tear the paper.

Install the ceiling sheets.

Hang drywall on the ceiling before installing the wall sheets. Start in a corner and against one side of the room and work out from there, keeping the panels perpendicular to the joists. Take time before you start to locate joists and mark their locations on the sheet and the wall. Searching for joists while holding the sheet up with your head is no fun.

The quickest, but most difficult, way to install drywall on a ceiling is to set the panel in place and support it with your head, leaving your hands free to hold and drive nails or screws. Wearing a baseball cap greatly minimizes pulled hair and a sore head.

To make things easier, construct one or two 2×2 T-braces to use as props. Or, rent a drywall hoist. Either solution will make the process easier and result in a much neater job.

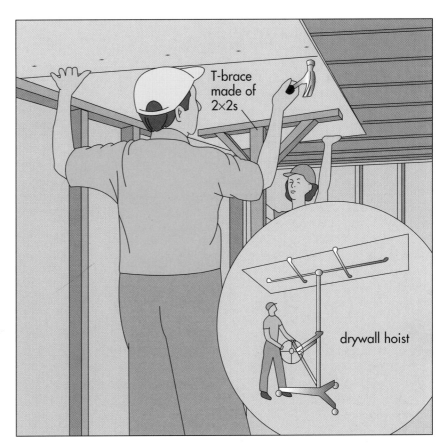

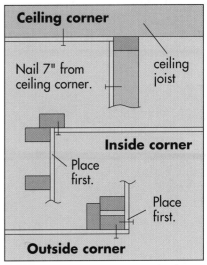

TOOLS TO USE

DRYWALL HAMMER

There are hammers made especially for drywall installation. They are light, for easy handling; they have wide heads so it's easier to make a dimple without damaging the paper; and their heads are tilted a bit for access into corners. You may not use one very often, but it will make hanging and, subsequently, taping easier.

DRYWALL SCREWDRIVER OR DIMPLER BIT

A drywall screwdriver has an adjustable bit that, once set correctly, will drive the bit to the correct depth, then stop. A less expensive, and just as good, option is a dimpler bit that you can attach to a drill.

Install the wall sheets.

Once the ceiling panels are up, hang sheets on the walls. If you are installing sheets horizontally, begin with the upper sheets, butting them firmly against the ceiling drywall. Make sure all vertical seams hit studs. Butt the lower panels firmly against the upper panels, tapered edge to tapered edge. Raise up sheets tightly with a wedge or lever.

If you are installing sheets

vertically, check the tapered edges to make sure they fall midway across a stud. If they don't, either cut the drywall or attach pieces of lumber to the stud to give yourself a nailing surface for the next piece.

Overlap pieces at corners, as shown *above*. Finish the job by adding the filler pieces, measuring and cutting each piece to size. Make sure each piece has at least two nailing members to support it.

TAPING DRYWALL

Once you've gained some experience, three coats of drywall compound, with sandings, will produce smooth walls. But as a beginner, don't be surprised if it takes you four or five coats. Unless you have large holes that require patching plaster, use ready-mixed drywall joint compound. Dry-mix compounds provide more strength for trouble areas, but you'll need to work fast if you use them. To hide imperfections, apply texture to your walls with a rented texture gun and hopper.

YOU'LL NEED

TIME: For a typical bedroom, 5 hours for the first coat and 2 hours for subsequent coats, plus time for sanding and drying.
SKILLS: Patience and willingness to learn.
TOOLS: Utility knife; 6-, 10-, and 12-inch taping blades; corner taping tool; pole sander or hand sander; tin snips.

EXPERTS' INSIGHT

DRYWALL FINISHING TIPS

■ Use self-sticking mesh tape on the drywall wherever a tapered edge meets a tapered edge, as shown *above*. Use paper tape everywhere else. Mesh tape requires less joint compound, but does not work as well for inside corners.
■ Rusty, gunked-up tools ruin your work. Scrape, wash, and dry blades after every use.
■ When sanding, control the extremely fine dust by using a fan to pull the dust out a window. Seal doorways and wear a breathing mask.

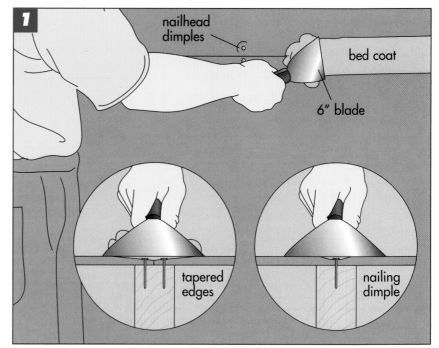

1. Apply a bed coat.
Conceal nailheads by putting compound on a 6-inch taping blade and passing over the spot twice. Make sure you leave compound only in the depression and none on the rest of the sheet. Do this with each coat until the dimple is filled in completely.

Joints are much more difficult—butt joints especially. If you are using self-sticking mesh tape, simply cut pieces to fit, press them into place, and begin applying joint compound. For paper tape, start by spreading a bed coat over the joint with a 6-inch taping blade. Apply just enough for the paper tape to adhere.

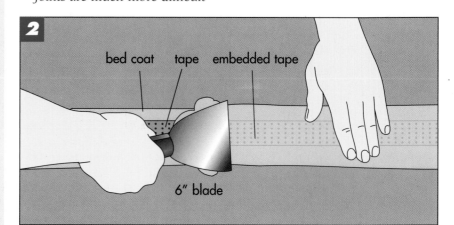

2. Embed the tape in compound.
(Skip this step if you are using mesh tape.) Immediately after applying the bed coat to a joint, center a length of paper tape over the joint and press the tape firmly against the filled joint by running your taping blade along it. If the tape begins to slide, hold it in place with your hand. If bubbles form under the tape, if there are places where the tape is not sticking to the bed coat, or if wrinkles appear, peel the tape back and apply more compound. Then press the tape back again.

3. Apply compound over the tape.

Load a 10-inch taping blade with compound and apply a smooth coat over the tape. Where two tapered joints meet, make sure the blade extends past both tapers. Fill in the tapers only, so you have a flat wall surface. For butt joints, feather out the compound 7 to 9 inches on each side; a small ridge in the middle can be sanded later. After the compound dries, scrape off ridges and bumps, and sand. Apply and sand successive coats until the surface is smooth.

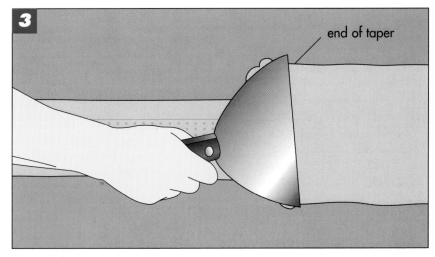

4. Coat outside corners.

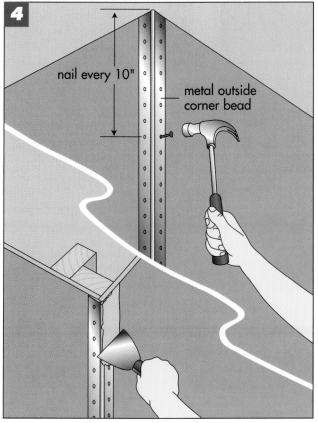

To protect and conceal the drywall edges that meet at an outside corner, cut a piece of metal corner bead using tin snips. Fit the strip over the corner and fasten it to the wall one side at a time. Drive in nails or screws at 10-inch intervals. Check to make sure the flange of the corner bead does not protrude above what will be the finished surface by running a taping blade along the length of the corner bead. Fasten down any areas of flange that protrude. Apply a coat of joint compound with a 6-inch blade angled away from the corner. Allow one side of the blade to ride on the bead, the other side on the wall. For subsequent coats, use 10- and 12-inch blades.

5. Tape inside corners.

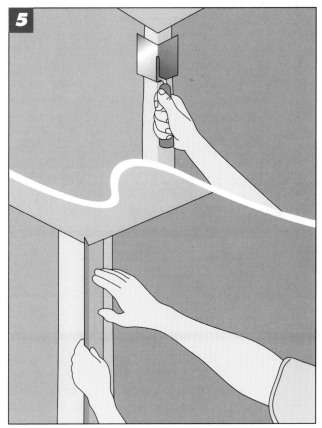

Outside corners can be almost fun, but inside corners are more difficult. Apply a bed coat of compound to both sides with a 6-inch blade. Cut a piece of paper tape to the correct length, fold it, and place it in position by hand. Keep it straight to avoid wrinkles. Run a corner taping tool along its length to embed the tape in the compound. Lift and reapply compound wherever the tape has wrinkles, bubbles, or nonadhering spots. Once the tape is embedded, apply some compound to the walls and some to the corner tool. Stroke on a smooth coat. This will take several passes and some practice. You may find it easier to feather out the edges with an 8-inch blade.

INSTALLING PANELING

Sheet paneling needs a solid, plumb backing. Typically, this is a stud wall covered with ½-inch drywall. On the inside of exterior and below-grade walls, sandwich insulation and a vapor barrier between the studs and the drywall to protect panels from moisture.

As you estimate materials, keep in mind that panel seams must hit studs. Lay out the job to avoid thin strips of paneling. It's better to cut 14 inches off the first panel on a wall than end up with a piece 2 inches wide at the end of the wall. Stand the panels up for 48 hours in the room in which they'll be installed to condition them.

YOU'LL NEED

TIME: About a day to panel a medium-size room.
SKILLS: Measuring, scribing, cutting sheets, nailing.
TOOLS: Level, hammer, nail set, caulking gun.

EXPERTS' INSIGHT

CHOOSING PANELING

Sheet paneling is inexpensive and easy to install, but it is also thin and flexible. If your walls are at all wavy, the paneling will accentuate the curves rather than hide them.

If you have problem walls, consider tongue-and-groove planks. They are more expensive and take longer to install, but they'll straighten the walls. Planking requires furring strips and shims every 16 vertical inches for backing.

Be sure to inspect sheet paneling for variations in color, flaws, and splinters.

1. Mark the seams.
Mark the location of the studs where the panel edges will meet. Cut the first sheet so its edge falls on the middle of a stud. Set the first piece in place without attaching it. Panels should have a ¹⁄₁₆-inch gap between them to allow for expansion and contraction. To disguise the gap, run a felt marker along the seam.

3. Tack the sheet in place.
Align the panel so it is plumb and drive three or more finish or color-matched paneling nails halfway in along the top edge of the panel. With the panel dangling, compress the adhesive behind it by hammering on the surface with a block of wood wrapped in cloth.

2. Apply adhesive.
Using a caulking gun, apply a ½-inch bead of panel adhesive on the wall in a wavy pattern so there is no gap larger than 8 inches between adhesive beads. (A large caulking gun that holds quart tubes may be a worthwhile investment.) Press the panel back in place and elevate it above the floor about ½ inch.

4. Let adhesive set, attach panel.
Pull out the bottom of the panel and insert a spacer to keep it away from the wall while the adhesive sets up. After the time specified for the adhesive (typically, 3 minutes), press the panel against the wall and drive in nails every 8 inches along the edges and every 12 inches into intermediate studs.

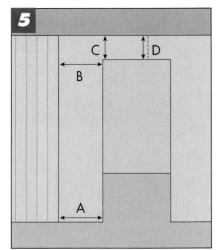

5. Panel around an opening.

To panel around a door or window, measure over from the last panel installed. Measure up from the floor or down from the ceiling to find the height of the opening. Measure in the A, B, C, D sequence shown. If possible, lay out panels so their seams fall over the center of openings. Remember to allow a 1/16-inch gap between the panels.

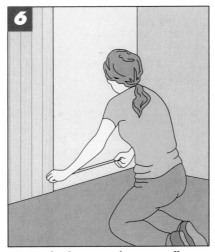

6. Fit the last panel on a wall.

For the last piece, you'll need to precision-cut a panel to fit neatly against the inside edge of the wall. Most likely, the corner will not be plumb, so measure from the previous panel to the corner at several points along the panel edge and draw a line with a straightedge. Cut with a circular saw or a sabersaw if the curves are pronounced. When cutting with either of these tools, flip the panel over so the finish side is down.

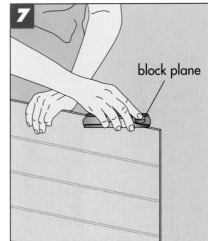

7. Fine-tune the edge.

It may take several attempts before you get a piece to fit against an irregular corner. Be conservative in your cutting; you can always cut more, but you can't make the sheet bigger. Use a block plane or surface-forming tool to shave off small amounts of material. Hold the tool at an angle so the bulk of the material is cut from the back of the panel, leaving a thin, easily trimmed edge at the surface for final fitting.

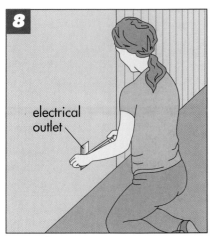

8. Make cutouts.

To cut openings for electrical outlets, measure the distance between the last panel installed and the right and left edges of the outlet. Then measure the distance from the floor to the outlet top and bottom, subtracting the height the panel will be off the floor. Transfer your measurements to the paneling and cut out the hole with a keyhole saw.

9. Cut around complex obstructions.

To cut around such structures as a fireplace and mantel, measure the distance from the last installed sheet to the farthest point along the structure. Measure the height of the structure, allowing for the gap along the floor. Transfer your measurements to the paneling, connect the cut lines with a straightedge, and saw out the bulk of the waste area.

Temporarily nail up the sheet so it is plumb and alongside the structure at the proper elevation. Set a compass (see page 34) to the width the sheet needs to move to meet the last one installed and scribe the contours onto the sheet.

Make the cut using a sabersaw with a fine-tooth blade or a coping saw. Fit the panel and make fine adjustments with a utility knife. Secure the panel in place.

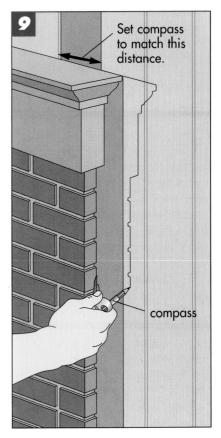

GLOSSARY

For words not listed here, or for more about those that are, refer to the index, pages 110–112.

Actual dimension. True size of a piece of lumber, after milling and drying. *See* **Nominal dimension.**

Awl. A sharp-pointed tool used for making small starter holes for screws or for scribing lines.

Batt. A section of fiberglass or rock-wool insulation measuring 15 or 23 inches wide by 4 to 8 feet long.

Bevel cut. A cut made at an angle through the thick dimension of a piece of wood.

Biscuit joiner. A mechanized tool used to cut incisions in lumber. Oval-shaped wooden biscuits are inserted into the incisions and glued to reinforce a joint.

Board. A piece of lumber that is less than 2 inches thick and more than 3 inches wide.

Board foot. The standard unit of measurement for wood. One board foot is equal to a piece 12×12×1 inches (nominal size).

Building codes. Community ordinances governing the manner in which a home or other structure may be constructed or modified. Most codes deal primarily with fire and health concerns and have separate sections relating to electrical, plumbing, and structural work.

Butt joint. A joint formed by two pieces of material when fastened end to end, end to face, or end to edge.

Casing. Trimming around a door, window, or other opening.

Chamfer. A bevel cut made along the length of a board edge.

Cleat. A length of board attached so as to strengthen or add support to a structure.

Clinch. To hammer the exposed tip of a nail at an angle, bending its point into the surrounding wood for added joint strength.

Coped cut. A profile cut made in the face of a piece of molding that allows for butting it against another piece at an inside corner.

Counterbore. To drive in a screw below the surface of the surrounding wood. The void created is filled later with putty or a wooden plug.

Countersink. To drive in the head of a nail or screw so its top is flush with the surface of the surrounding wood.

Crosscut. To saw a piece of lumber perpendicular to its length and/or its grain.

Dado joint. A joint formed when the end of one member fits into a groove cut partway through the face of another member.

Dimension lumber. A piece of lumber that is 2 inches thick and at least 2 inches wide.

Dowel. A piece of small-diameter wood rod used to reinforce joints.

Edging. Strips of wood or veneer used to cover the edges of plywood or boards.

End grain. The ends of wood fibers that are exposed at the ends of boards.

Filler. A pastelike compound used to hide surface imperfections in wood. One type, pore filler, levels the surface of wood that has a coarse grain.

Fire blocking. Short horizontal members sometimes nailed between framing studs, usually about halfway up the wall. They serve to slow a fire from moving up the framing space.

Flush. On the same plane as, or level with, a surrounding surface.

Furring. Lightweight strips of wood applied to walls to provide a plumb nailing surface for paneling or drywall.

Grain. The direction of fibers in a piece of wood; also refers to the pattern of the fibers.

Gusset. A piece of wood nailed or screwed over a joint to give it added strength.

Hardwood. Lumber derived from deciduous trees, such as oaks, maples, and walnuts.

Header. The framing component spanning a door or window opening in a wall. A header supports the weight above it and serves as a nailing surface for the door or window frame.

Inside corner. The point at which two walls form an internal angle, as in the corner of a room.

Jamb. The top and side frames of a door or window opening.

Joists. Horizontal framing members that support a floor and/or ceiling.

Kerf. The void created by the blade of a saw as it cuts through a piece of material.

Lag screw. A screw, usually ¼ inch in diameter or larger, with a hexagonal head that can be screwed in with an adjustable or socket wrench.

Lap joint. The joint formed when one member overlaps another.

Ledger. A horizontal strip (typically lumber) used to provide support for the ends or edges of other members.

Level. The condition that exists when a surface is at true horizontal. Also a tool used to determine level.

Linear foot. A term used to refer to the length of a board or piece of molding, in contrast to board foot.

Miter joint. The joint formed when two members meet that have been cut at the same angle, usually 45 degrees.

Molding. A strip of wood, usually small-dimensioned, used to cover exposed edges or as a decoration.

Mortise. A shallow cutout in a board, usually used to recess hardware, such as hinges.

Nominal dimension. The stated size of a piece of lumber, such as a 2×4 or a 1×12. The actual dimension is somewhat smaller.

On-center (OC). A term used to designate the distance from the center of one regularly spaced framing member to the center of the next one.

Outside corners. The point at which two walls form an external angle; the corner you usually can walk around.

Particleboard. Panels made from compressed wood chips and glue.

Pilot hole. A small hole drilled into a wooden member to avoid splitting the wood when driving in a screw or nail.

Plumb. The condition that exists when a member is at true vertical.

Pressure-treated wood. Lumber and sheet goods impregnated with one of several solutions to make the wood more impervious to moisture and weather.

Rabbet. A step-shaped cut made along the edge of a piece of wood used to join boards tightly.

Rip. To saw lumber or sheet goods parallel to its grain pattern.

Roughing-in. The framing stage of a carpentry project. This framework later is concealed in the finishing stages.

Rout. To shape edges or cut grooves using a router.

Sealer. A protective, usually clear, coating applied to wood or metal.

Setting nails. Driving in the heads of nails slightly below the surface of the wood.

Shim. A thin strip or wedge of wood or other material used to fill a gap between two adjoining components or to help establish level or plumb.

Soffit. Covering attached to the underside of eaves or a staircase.

Softwood. Lumber derived from coniferous trees, such as pines, firs, cedars, or redwoods.

Square. The condition that exists when one surface is at a 90-degree angle to another. Also a tool used to determine square.

Studs. Vertical 2×4 or 2×6 framing members spaced at regular intervals within a wall.

Taper. A gradual and uniform decrease in the width or thickness of a board.

Taping. The process of covering drywall joints with paper tape and joint compound.

Three-four-five method. An easy, mathematical way to check whether a corner of a large area is square. Measure 3 feet along one side and 4 feet along the other. If the corner is square, the diagonal distance between those two points will equal 5 feet.

Toenail. To drive a nail at an angle to hold together two pieces of material, usually studs in a wall.

Tongue-and-groove joint. A joint made using boards that have a projecting tongue on the end of one member and a corresponding groove on the other member into which the tongue fits.

Top plate. The topmost horizontal element of a stud-frame wall.

Vapor barrier. A waterproof membrane in a floor, wall, or ceiling that blocks the transfer of condensation to the inner surface.

Veneer. A thin layer of decorative wood laminated to the surface of a more common wood.

Warp. Any of several lumber defects caused by uneven shrinkage of wood cells.

INDEX

A–B

Adhesives
for furring strips, 99
for laminate, 61
for paneling, 60, 106
selecting, 25, 60
Anchors, 55
Angle brackets, 26
Angle cuts, 34, 37–38
Antiquing, 71
Awls, 8, 54
Backsaws, 8, 9
Basements, 98–99, 101
Bench grinders, 13
Beveled cuts, 38, 49, 50
Biscuit joiners, 12–13, 65
Bits, drill
damage to, 45
for locksets, 89
for screws, 54
types of, 44, 46–47, 89, 103
Board feet, 16
Bolts, 25, 55–56
Braces, 47
Brackets, 26, 84
Building codes, 4, 102

C

Cabinets
base, 76, 79
choosing, 76
hardware, 26–27
installing, 78–79
planning for new, 76–77
wall, 76, 78, 84–85
Catches, 26–27
Cat's paws, 10, 57
Caulking, 10, 60
Ceilings, drywalling, 102, 103
Chalk lines, 8
Chisels, 8–9, 42–43, 82, 88
Chopsaws. *See* Miter saws, power
Circular saws, 11, 36–38, 43
Clamps, 8, 9–10, 59
Closet organizing systems, 81
Compass techniques, 34–35
Contour cuts, 34, 40–41
Coping saws, 8, 9, 41, 75
Countersink bits, 44, 46
Countertop installation, 80
Crosscuts, 39, 48, 50, 100
Cutoff lines, 29–30
Cutouts, 30, 39, 101, 107

D

Dadoes
blades for, 49
chiseling, 43, 82
radial-arm saws and, 50
for shelves, 82–83
tablesaws and, 49
Deadbolt locks, 89–90
Doors
cutting, 87
hanging, 88, 90
hardware, 26–27
headers, 6, 7, 95
hinges, 26–27, 86–88
locks, 26–27, 88–90
planing, 86
prehung, 90, 95
removing, 86
roughing-in opening for, 95
scribing bottom of, 34
shimming, 86–87
sticking or squeaking, 86–87
strike plates, 87, 89
Dowels, 62, 65
Drawer slides, 26–27
Drilling
ceramic tile, 47
concrete, 47
guides for, 45
for locks, 89–90
masonry, 47
metal, 47
pilot holes, 25, 53–54
starter holes, 45
techniques, 44, 45–47
Drills. *See also* Bits, drill
choosing, 44
damage to, 45
power, 11, 13, 44
presses, 13
stands, 12, 13
Drywall
attaching to metal framing, 97
in basements, 101
building codes for, 102
on ceilings, 102–103
compound, 104–105
cutting, 40, 100–101
finishing tips, 104
handling and storing, 23, 100
hanging, 102–103
laying out, 100
nails, 24, 102
screws, 25, 55, 102
selecting, 20, 21
squares, 10, 32, 100, 101
taping, 104–105
tools, 8, 9–10, 103

E–G

Electrical receptacles, 77
Exterior carpentry terms, 6–7
Files, 8, 9
Fillers and filling, 70
Finishes and finishing, 70–71
Framing
building of, 91–94
house anatomy and, 6–7
I-beams and, 96
lumber for, 17
members for doors, 95
metal, 96–97
pipes and, 96
squares, 8, 9, 31
Furring basement walls, 98–99
Gluing, 59–60
Ground-fault circuit interrupters
(GFCIs), 77

H–I

Hammers
drywall, 103
power, 99
selecting, 8, 9
using, 52–53
Handsaws, 8, 9, 39
Hand tools, 8–10. *See also* specific
hand tools
Hanger screws, 25
Hardware
cabinet, 26–27
door, 26–27
shelf, 26, 84
Headers, 6, 7, 95
Hinges
installing, 88
mortises for, 43, 88
remounting, 86
rusty, 87
selecting, 26–27
Holes, filling, 70
Holesaws, 44
House anatomy, 6–7

J–L

Joints
biscuit, 63, 65
butt, 62
dado, 63–64
dowel, 62, 65
half-lap, 63–64

METRIC CONVERSIONS

U.S. UNITS TO METRIC EQUIVALENTS			METRIC UNITS TO U.S. EQUIVALENTS		
To Convert From	Multiply By	To Get	To Convert From	Multiply By	To Get
Inches	25.4	Millimetres	Millimetres	0.0394	Inches
Inches	2.54	Centimetres	Centimetres	0.3937	Inches
Feet	30.48	Centimetres	Centimetres	0.0328	Feet
Feet	0.3048	Metres	Metres	3.2808	Feet
Yards	0.9144	Metres	Metres	1.0936	Yards
Miles	1.6093	Kilometres	Kilometres	0.6214	Miles
Square inches	6.4516	Square centimetres	Square centimetres	0.1550	Square inches
Square feet	0.0929	Square metres	Square metres	10.764	Square feet
Square yards	0.8361	Square metres	Square metres	1.1960	Square yards
Acres	0.4047	Hectares	Hectares	2.4711	Acres
Square miles	2.5899	Square kilometres	Square kilometres	0.3861	Square miles
Cubic inches	16.387	Cubic centimetres	Cubic centimetres	0.0610	Cubic inches
Cubic feet	0.0283	Cubic metres	Cubic metres	35.315	Cubic feet
Cubic feet	28.316	Litres	Litres	0.0353	Cubic feet
Cubic yards	0.7646	Cubic metres	Cubic metres	1.308U	Cubic yards
Cubic yards	764.55	Litres	Litres	0.0013	Cubic yards
Fluid ounces	29.574	Millilitres	Millilitres	0.0338	Fluid ounces
Quarts	0.9464	Litres	Litres	1.0567	Quarts
Gallons	3.7854	Litres	Litres	0.2642	Gallons
Drams	1.7718	Grams	Grams	0.5644	Drams
Ounces	28.350	Grams	Grams	0.0353	Ounces
Pounds	0.4536	Kilograms	Kilograms	2.2046	Pounds
To convert from degrees Fahrenheit (F) to degrees Celsius (C), first subtract 32, then multiply by 5/9.			To convert from degrees Celsius to degrees Fahrenheit, multiply by 9/5, then add 32.		